"The secular and scientific age in which we live demands that things be tested and re-tested. They require evidence upon evidence, fact upon fact. Yet here in the truest sense is a controlled experiment. Christianity has been observed for almost a thousand years. Wherever it is faithfully proclaimed, accepted, and acted upon, it transforms men, cultures, and societies; and it can do this only because it is energized by a living Savior.

"Inscribed upon the tomb of the great architect Christopher Wren is this statement, 'If you would see the man's monument, look around.' Well might we say this in an infinitely greater sense of Jesus Christ, for through the centuries He has established living monuments to His power to save, miraculously transforming the lives of those who would dare to believe the incredible.

"To those who come to Him, Jesus Christ becomes the solution to all the problems of soul and body. The results of their experience with Him become the truly unanswerable argument of essential Christianity."

—Dr. Walter Martin

ESSENTIAL CHRISTIANITY

ESSENTIAL CHRISTIANITY

DR. WALTER MARTIN

A HANDBOOK OF BASIC CHRISTIAN DOCTRINES

Regal Books
A Division of GL Publications
Ventura, California, U.S.A.

Published by Regal Books
A Division of Gospel Light
Ventura, California 93006
Printed in U.S.A.

Regal Books is a ministry of Gospel Light, an evangelical Christian publisher dedicated to serving the local church. We believe God's vision for
Gospel Light is to provide church leaders with biblical, user-friendly mate-
rials that will help them evangelize, disciple and minister to children,
youth and families.

It is our prayer that this Regal Book will help you discover biblical truth
for your own life and help you meet the needs of others. May God rich-
ly bless you.

*For a free catalog of resources from Regal Books/Gospel Light please contact
your Christian supplier or call 1-800-4-GOSPEL.*

Except where otherwise indicated, all Scripture quotations are taken from
the King James Version of the Bible.

ESSENTIAL CHRISTIANITY
Copyright © 1962, 1975, 1980 by Walter R. Martin

Revised 1975, 1980 by Walter R. Martin

Library of Congress Catalog No. 80-51625
ISBN No. 0-8307-1029-9

10 11 12 13 14 15 16 17 18 / KP / 99 98 97 96 95 94

Rights for publishing this book in other languages are contracted by Gospel Literature
International (GLINT). GLINT also provides technical help for the adaptation, translation,
and publishing of Bible study resources and books in scores of languages worldwide. For
further information, contact GLINT, Post Office Box 4060, Ontario, California, 91761-1003,
U.S.A., or the publisher.

To
EDWARD D. THAYER
and the New York City Bible Class, who faithfully supported and encouraged me in the
preparation and publication of these lectures,
this volume is affectionately dedicated.

ACKNOWLEDGMENTS

The author wishes to thank the late Pierson Curtis, former senior master of Stony Brook School, who greatly assisted in the editing and proofreading of this manuscript, and the Rev. Anthony Collarile, who aided me in documentary research.

CONTENTS

PREFACE

The purpose of this volume is to provide for Christians and non-Christians alike a brief introductory survey of the essential foundations of Christian theology. It is not designed to be a complete study of all Biblical doctrines.

Christianity of course is far more than just a series of doctrinal propositions or a code of moral and ethical conduct, since one can be a non-Christian and have all of these ingredients. Christianity is first and foremost the Person of the Savior, Jesus Christ, His nature and His work for "us men and our salvation." Apart from union with Him by faith and the transforming power and presence of His grace in the life, one either embraces the form of what is a dead orthodoxy apart from the Christian ethic and love, or a counterfeit ethic and love devoid of sound Biblical doctrine. These are unattractive alternatives to true redemption, but they are two prominent camps all too apparent in the Christian world today.

We have conducted our study on the basis of one major Biblical assumption, namely, the truth that it is the Word of God. Volumes have been written, are being written, and will yet be written to prove this thesis, and many dissenting voices have been heard and will be heard in the future.

Dr. Frank Gaebelein has stated my position when he said, "As Christians we cannot afford to have a view of the Scriptures lower than that held by our Lord, who declared that 'the Scriptures cannot be broken' and 'thy Word is truth.'" The Bible therefore is the source of all the doctrines reviewed in this book, and its veracity and integrity are granted even as "the foundation of God stands sure."

The only unshakable foundations, then, are the teachings of God Himself, and while one day He will "shake the heavens and the earth," only the things which are temporal will vanish away — the things which are unseen and eternal will remain. The faith of the church has always been one of the things unseen since it is by nature "the substance of things hoped for, the evidence of things invisible."

It is the prayer of the author that through this modest effort, a handbook of essential doctrines, the reader may catch a glimpse of the Master Builder of all creation and of His indescribable grace, which has built us upon "the foundation of the apostles and prophets, Jesus Christ himself being the chief corner *stone*" (Ephesians 2:20; cf. 1 Peter 2:3-8).

—WALTER MARTIN
San Juan Capistrano, California
March 1980

1

THY WORD IS TRUTH

More than thirty-five years ago, over the door of a small brick chapel, I first saw the sentence "Thy Word is Truth" (John 17:17). The chapel belonged to the Stony Brook School on Long Island. Here, as a religious but agnostic teenager, I had been sent into social exile by my parents. It was not that they wanted to isolate me from society (for Stony Brook School was far from such an isolation), but simply that they wanted me to be disciplined in both intellect and will. And what better place could I be sent, they reasoned, than to a school that had as its motto "Character before Career"?

It was at Stony Brook School (then, as now, a bastion of evangelical Christianity) that I first came to know Him "of whom Moses in the law, and the prophets, did write, Jesus of Nazareth . . ." (John 1:45).

It was necessary for me as part of my education at Stony Brook to study the Bible, which I had always regarded with respect but never in the light of absolute spiritual authority. With the brash skepticism of youth and inexperience, I questioned everything I read and plagued my teachers, including the learned headmaster Dr. Frank Gaebelein, with literally hundreds of questions. The end product of this quest was a journey from doubt to faith, accompanied by the fruit of genuine faith — an enduring experience with God.

It is therefore possible for me to understand the mind of the skeptic, the agnostic, and the professional scoffer, since I have worn all their boots at one time or another and have followed the same old arguments to their dismal and fruitless conclusion — the absurdity of life and the purposelessness of existence apart from the living God. In the brief span of this chapter it is impossible, of course, to treat in depth the subject of Biblical inspiration. In the final analysis, "He that cometh to God must believe that he is, and that he is a rewarder of them that diligently seek him" (Hebrews 11:6). No amount of argument or evidence conjured or amassed by the human mind can convince a skeptic that God has spoken, until God has been permitted to speak to him. If, as the Bible teaches, the soul of man is a locked door, the handle being inside, so that the knock of God must be responded to from within, then ultimately it will be His grace alone which enables us to turn the key and the handle so that the light of heaven may illumine the darkness of our sins.

This chapter, then, is not intended to be an exhaustive apologetic for the inspiration or authenticity of the Bible. Rather, it is an attempt to answer some questions which are frequently asked about the Scriptures, and to set forth in clear, nontechnical language precisely what the Christian church means when it speaks about the authority and inspiration of divine revelation. Many excellent works have been written which point out the historical accuracy and prophetic validity of Biblical data.[1] The science of archeology has in the last hundred years confirmed in startling detail what patient scholars of the Bible have always believed — that it is an enormously reliable book, completely trustworthy, and remarkably relevant.[2]

What do we mean, then, when we say, "The Bible is the Word of God"? It is obvious that we are asserting that the Bible is a revelation from God — that it does not just illumine our thinking but reveals to our minds things which God knows and which we are incapable of learning apart from His communication with us.

What we mean when we talk about the Bible as the Word of God is that it is a compilation of 66 books which span a period of more than 5,000 years and were written by multiple authors, all of whom testify to the fact that they had an experience with a spiritual Being whom they described as "the Lord" or "the Eternal One." It therefore cannot be asserted logically that the Christian is arguing in a circle because he allegedly quotes the Bible to prove the Bible, as some critics maintain. The Bible is not *one* book but many, written by people of different time periods, all of whom bear witness to their relationship with an ultradimensional Being who lives outside our time-space continuum — a Being who wishes us to know that He is our Creator and desires to be our loving heavenly Father.

The error arises when we think of the Bible as *one* book, since in reality it is a *collection* of books. The testimony of the authors must be accepted as independent evidence unless it can be shown conclusively that there was either collusion or deception on their part. It should be strongly emphasized that such collusion has never been proven — in fact, quite the opposite is the case.

Since the Bible is a collection of books, it contains quotations from men (Acts 17:28), angels (Matthew 1:20), demons (Mark 5:9), Satan (Job 1:9), and God Himself (Exodus 20:1 ff.). However, the Bible is called the Word of *God* because the whole transcript is an inspired, faithful, and infallible record of what God intended us to know about Himself, the cosmos in which we live, our spiritual allies and adversaries, and our fellow man. The Bible, then, was produced by men whose recording of events was divinely supervised and preserved from all the frailties of human error and judgment which are so common in all other religious literature.

How could such faithful recording come about? By what

method could God bring such a thing to pass? Such questions can be answered simply by pointing out an illustration from the late Donald Grey Barnhouse. Dr. Barnhouse maintained that, even as the Holy Spirit came upon the womb of the Virgin Mary and, despite her sinful nature, imperfections, and limitations, produced the sinless and perfect character who is called the Son of God, so He moved upon the minds and spirits of the recorders of Scripture that, despite limitations in language, culture, and even scientific knowledge, He produced His perfect message to mankind. Both phenomena were miraculous; both were perfect births — one of the Son of Man and the other of a Book, the Word of God. When we speak of the inspiration of the Scriptures, then, we are talking about the process that God used to convey His message. This process is described by the Apostle Paul as a type of spiritual "breathing." In fact, the Greek word *theopneustos* literally means "God-breathed."

The inspiration of the Bible and the concepts just mentioned refer only to the initial "breathing" of God upon the authors of Scripture to produce a copy of His thoughts for man. It is for this original text of Scripture, revealed by God and faithfully recorded by His servants, that the Christian church claims infallibility. Through the centuries God has preserved literally thousands of copies and fragments of these initial manuscripts with only minor transmissional mistakes made by scribes over the years. Historic Christianity affirms the plenary or "full" inspiration of the Bible, and it further holds that inspired concepts can be communicated only by inspired words. Thus, the church's belief in the *verbal* inspiration of the Bible is logically inseparable from the doctrine of plenary inspiration.

To illustrate, the label on all RCA records contained a picture of a dog listening to an old Victrola with the caption "His Master's Voice." Dr. Eugene Nida of the translation department of the American Bible Society has pointed out that the dog listening to the Victrola will hear an imperfect transmission of his master's voice because the needle scratches the surface of the record.

However, no matter how scratchy the record sounds, the needle cannot obliterate the sound of the master's voice — the message still comes through.

Expanding on this concept a little more, we can see that the Bible is represented by the record and that the imperfections of human nature and the limitations of human knowledge are represented by the needle. The passage of time is represented by the turntable. Just as any record becomes scratchy in time through wear, so is this true (though in a lesser degree) with the copies of Scripture. But in spite of these limitations (the direct product of human freedom and its resultant sin), we can still hear our Master's voice, just as the dog does on the record label. The "scratches" are also being "erased" as time goes on by archeology, by older and better texts, and by scientific discoveries. More of the "original" is thus being "dubbed" back into the copies, so that year by year we are getting closer to the "master tape" from which all the duplicates (copies of manuscripts) were recorded. Thus the accuracy of our Bible copies *increases* rather than decreases. The clarity of the message improves steadily with the passage of time, and the fidelity of our Master's voice is now growing clearer and clearer.

Let us never forget the fact that a hundred years ago the percentage of "questionable" textual material existing in the then-available copies of the Bible was approximately *five times greater* than that which raises questions for critical scholarship today. This is positive proof that the situation is *not* static but is very much alive and is moving in the direction of *resolving* textual and critical problems instead of multiplying them. Because of advancing knowledge about the Bible and its times, great gains have been made in solving problems which a hundred years ago were considered by some reputable scholars to be "insoluble." Thus it would be foolish indeed to abandon faith in the authority of God's initial revelation simply because there remains a relatively small percentage (less than ½ of 1 percent in the New Testament) of questionable material about which we do not yet have enough data to properly evaluate and understand. Those who gave up their faith in the absolute authority of Scripture a hundred years ago (as well as their disciples today) would do well to remember that advancing truth *confirms* rather than diminishes the accuracy and authority of the Bible. God has a long record of blessing those who believe Him and who believe in the integrity of what He has said. He has yet to raise up a great evangelist, Bible teacher, or pastor from the ranks of those evangelicals who maintain that human error exists in the original documents of Scripture.

Two other questions are perennially raised regarding copies of the Bible, and they are worthy of a studied answer. First, if copies of the Bible reveal error, why can we not infer that the originals contained the same errors? There is, of course, a sound answer to at least part of this question. Since no one has the original autographs or "master tape" of the Bible, we can just as logically infer the opposite — that the apparent errors we now observe were not errors in the original at all, but were errors of inaccurate transcription. Both positions are essentially arguments from silence, and the solution probably lies elsewhere. However, one note should be made — the argument that assumes error in the original manuscripts is based on the belief that what exists in a copy will also exist in the original, if found. This is a negative faith, since its conclusion includes doubt of the prophets and the apostles. The position which maintains by faith (and with steadily mounting evidence) that the original manuscripts are errorless exemplifies *positive* faith in the complete reliability of the prophets and the apostles and in the trustworthiness of their initial transcription of the data they received from God.

Secondly, why would God inspire free of error the original autograph or "master" copy of the Biblical record (from which all subsequent copies are made) and then permit the copies to become even minutely corrupted in transmission? Would this not defeat His whole original purpose — an infallible record?

The answer to this question lies in a correct understanding of the nature of the freedom of the will. Adam was created innocent, and God put His divine stamp of approval on that creation by calling him "the son of God" (Luke 3:38). So in like manner He put His seal upon the Scriptures when He first gave them by calling them "My Word" more than 3,000 times.

Jesus Christ also held the very highest view of Scripture (John 12:44-50; 17:17), for it was He who said, "the Scriptures cannot be broken" (John 10:35). Those who would own Him as their Master cannot in good conscience hold a view of Scripture inferior to His.

Even though Adam was created innocent, by an act of free will he fell into imperfect practices which God allowed so as not to violate the freedom which alone makes it possible for men and angels to choose to love Him. This was extended by necessity and nature to the sons of Adam, some of whom later copied and recopied the divine record. Their errors, however, are *not* to be considered God's Word, nor does God extend His divine seal of approval to any human error. What is truly remarkable is that no transmissional error has ever affected a single doctrine of the Word of God which touches the means of our salvation, the evangelization of the world, our own spiritual maturity, or the church's ultimate conquest of evil.

The Word of God is God in His Word, speaking to us by His Spirit, through whom the message was initially inspired and infused into the souls and minds of His servants. These "holy men of God spake *as they were* moved by the Holy Ghost" (2 Peter 1:18-21). Speaking through the prophets, God bore record in the Old Testament of the coming Messiah, Jesus Christ the Living Word. In the New Testament God testifies to the apostles and the disciples of the Incarnation of His Word (John 1:1,14). These truths are confirmed experientially by the witness of the Holy Spirit, who carries on the work of confronting men with the written Word, which points them to the living Word. It is the Holy Spirit who validates the witness by transforming those who accept the Bible's testimony to the risen Christ, our only object of saving faith. Is it any wonder that Peter could proclaim of the Lord Jesus, "To him give all the prophets witness, that through his name whosoever believeth in him shall receive remission of sins" (Acts 10:43)!

Thus the Holy Spirit, who inspired the written Word and who anointed the Living Word, perseveres in validating all His work of inspiration through the fulfillment of prophecy and the transformation of lives in response to faith in the Lord Jesus. The action of the Holy Spirit in and upon the sons of Adam is a living reminder to the church that our "labor is not in vain in the Lord."

There are still problems and questions to be answered in both the Old and New Testament. Though small in number, there still exist apparent contradictions and confusing chronologies. One cannot read the synoptic Gospels without becoming aware of the fact that there is an insufficiency of data to solve some of the problems which are raised by literary and textual criticism. We must not forget, however, that insufficiency of data does not at all logically postulate the existence of error. Rather, as we now know, what one hundred years ago was considered to be error by some liberal scholars is today regarded as factual data by even the most liberal Biblical scholars.[3]

The testimony of archeologists of the caliber of the late William F. Albright, Nelson Glueck, Cyrus Gordon, and Yigal Yadin cannot be ignored in any fair evaluation of Biblical accuracy and reliability. The evidence is in favor of the historic position of the church. When God speaks, there is no "indistinct sound" (1 Corinthians 14:8 NASB)—the Author of the ages does not stutter.

". . . thou hast magnified thy word above all thy name. . . . The word of God . . . liveth and abideth for ever" (Psalm 138:2; 1 Peter 1:23).

The words of the great Anglican scholar Bishop E. H. Bickersteth sum up the ancient and defensible position of historic

Christianity concerning the Bible. We would do well to listen prayerfully to his wisdom and believe in the truth he champions so well.

> In its sacred characters God speaks, and man speaks. Who can lay bare the mystery? Who can dissect the mingled shadings of the colours of the rainbow?

> But this inspiration of Scripture, though perfectly consistent with the individuality of the several writers, is altogether inconsistent with those rationalistic theories which subvert the faith of some in the present day. It absolutely refuses to allow the existence of anything false, or fallible, or merely human in the Scriptures as first given by God to man. Then should we need yet another revelation to assure us what was inspired and what uninspired, what was fallible and what infallible, what was human and what Divine. Further, it positively resists the theory of human reason, or any verifying faculty in man, being the ultimate judge of God's revelation. "For the prerogative of God," says Bacon, "extendeth as well to the reason as to the will of man; so that, we are to obey His law, though we find a reluctation in our will. So are we to believe His words, though we find a reluctation in our reason. For if we believe only what is agreeable to our sense, we give consent to the matter, not to the Author, which is no more than we do to a suspected and discredited witness. Nor ought we to draw down or submit the mysteries of God to our reason, but, contrariwise, to raise and advance our reason to the Divine truth.

> This obedience of faith does not in the very least interfere with the useful and important duty of critical investigation. Though, in better words than my own, "Let us always be cautious that we do not extend criticism beyond its limits. To investigate the merits of copies and versions; to lead us up by a careful process of inquiry to the very text, as near as may be, as it was penned by the various authors; to illustrate what they have said, and to facilitate the understanding of their words — this is the object, this the ample field of sacred criticism. But an awful responsibility is incurred if we elevate it into the judge of prophets and apostles, to censure them for what they *have* said, and to pronounce what they should have said; to declare their reasoning inconclusive, and their statements inaccurate; to regard them as led astray with false philosophy, and bewildered for want of recollection; to thrust them, in fact, far below a shrewd professor in a German university, who could have taught the world more skillfully than they did—from this the devout mind should intuitively shrink. We are commanded, indeed, to prove all things; we are encouraged by the book itself to search whether the things it tells us be so. But surely the authenticity and general truthfulness of the record being established, its own testimony is sufficient to indicate its highest claims."

> These claims—to sum up what I have said before—are nothing less than the plenary inspiration of Scripture, from Genesis to Malachi, from Matthew to Revelation. Every jot and tittle of the Bible, as originally

penned by the sacred writers, is God's WORD WRITTEN—I repeat, as originally penned, for the truth here affirmed does not ask us to believe in the inspiration of copyists or translators or interpreters. Superficial errors, though we believe them to be few and comparatively unimportant, may have crept in during the lapse of ages. But the autographs were perfect. They may record the ungodly sayings and sentiments of ungodly men, but those sayings are historically true, and it was the mind of the Spirit thus to record them. They may embody earlier uninspired documents; but, if it be so, the fact of the Holy Ghost moving the sacred writers to embody them proves that every word is true, and stamps every sentence thus taken into the canon of Scripture with the seal of God. They do in their various parts bear the unmistakable impress of the individual character of every author (for inspiration is not of necessity dictation), but each one spake as he was moved by the Holy Ghost. So the one inspiring breath of the [pipe] organ gives forth the sound, which the conformation of every pipe impresses on it. It is God speaking to man in man's language. And as the Incarnate Word was subject to the innocent infirmities of humanity, though absolutely and perfectly without sin, so the written Word is the mind of God, couched in the feeble symbolism of human speech, but yet is pure, perfect, and infallible. This glorious possession — this choicest heirloom of the family of man — we owe to the inspiration of the Holy Ghost.[4]

CHAPTER NOTES

1. For further information on prophecy and the historicity of the Bible, see Werner Keller, *The Bible as History* (New York: William Morrow & Co., 1956, 1964); Josh McDowell, *Evidence That Demands a Verdict* (San Bernardino, CA: Campus Crusade for Christ, 1972, 1979); and Josh McDowell, *More Evidence That Demands a Verdict* (San Bernardino, CA: Campus Crusade for Christ, 1975).

2. For further information on archaeology and the reliability of the Bible, see E.M. Blaiklock, *The Archaeology of the New Testament* (Grand Rapids: Zondervan, 1970, 1974); William Foxwell Albright, *From the Stone Age to Christianity* (Garden City, NY: Doubleday & Co., 1957); and Joseph P. Free, *Archaeology and Bible History* (Wheaton, IL: Scripture Press, 1950, 1962, 1969).

3. See Edwin R. Thiele, *A Cronology of the Hebrew Kings* (Grand Rapids: Zondervan, 1977); John A.T. Robinson, *Can We Trust the New Testament?* (Grand Rapids: Eerdmans, 1977); and John A.T. Robinson, *Redating the New Testament* (Philadelphia: Westminster Press, 1976).

4. Edward Henry Bickersteth, *The Holy Spirit: His Person and Work* (Grand Rapids: Kregel Publications, 1959, 1976), pp. 98-101.

2

GOD IN THREE PERSONS

No man can fully explain the Trinity, though in every age scholars have propounded theories and advanced hypotheses to explore this mysterious Biblical teaching. But despite the worthy efforts of these scholars, the Trinity is still largely incomprehensible to the mind of man.

Perhaps the chief reason for this is that the Trinity is a-logical, or beyond logic. It, therefore, cannot be made subject to human reason or logic. Because of this, opponents of the doctrine argue that the idea of the Trinity must be rejected as untenable. Such thinking, however, makes man's corrupted human reason the sole criterion for determining the truth of divine revelation.

God cannot be judged by man, nor can God's revelation be replaced by man's reason, and it is in God's revelation that we find the remarkable evidence for the Trinity in the Christian faith.

As the New Testament was completed toward the close of the first century, the infant church was struggling for its life against old foes — persecution and doctrinal error. On the one hand were the Roman Empire, orthodox Judaism, and hostile pagan religions, and on the other hand were heresies and divisive doctrines. Early Christianity was indeed a perilous experiment.

Probably no doctrine was the subject of more controversy in the early church than that of the Trinity. Certainly the teaching of "one God in three Persons" was accepted in the early church, but only as this teaching was challenged did a systematic doctrine of the Trinity emerge.

The Gnostic heresy, for instance, (which permeated Christendom in the lifetime of the apostles) drew strong condemnation in Paul's Epistle to the Colossians and John's First Epistle. Denying the deity of Christ, the Gnostics taught that He was inferior in nature to the Father, a type of super-angel or impersonal emanation from God.

Following the Gnostics came such speculative theologians as Origen, Lucian of Antioch, Paul of Samosota, Sabellius, and Arius of Alexandria. All of these propagated unbiblical views of the Trinity and of the divinity of our Lord.

But perhaps the most crucial test of Christian doctrine in the early church was the "Arian heresy." It was this heresy which stimulated the crystallization of thought regarding both the Trinity and the deity of Christ. The climax was reached at the famous Council of Nicea (325 A.D.). There, backed by laborious study of both Testaments, Athanasius and Paul (Bishop of Alexandria) decimated the Arian position and forced the excommunication of the schismatic Arius and his followers. At this time the church drafted the famed Nicene Creed and shortly afterward the Athanasian Creed. Thus the church recognized what the apostles and prophets had always taught — that the Messiah shares the nature of God, as does the Holy Spirit — "neither confounding the Persons nor dividing the Substance."

The Arians, on the other hand, never considered the matter a closed issue. As years passed, they almost split the Christian church apart, but time and time again they were thwarted by the great Athanasius, who held to the Scriptures tenaciously. Once, when he was hopelessly outnumbered, Athanasius was urged to join the Arians, and it was here that his character and that of the faithful Christians of the early church shone most brightly. With the challenge "The world is against you, Athanasius" ringing in his ears, the beleaguered theologian thundered, "No, it is not the world against me, it is Athanasius against the world." History records that though he lost many battles, he outlived Arius and won the final victory. Never again was the trinity of God successfully challenged within the church.

Today there are still remnants of the Gnostic heresy (Christian Science), the Arian heresy (Jehovah's Witnesses), and the Socinian heresy (Unitarianism) circulating in Christendom. All of these errors have one thing in common — they give Christ every title except the one which entitles Him to all the rest — the title of God and Savior.

But the Christian doctrine of the Trinity did not "begin" at the Council of Nicea, nor was it derived from "pagan influences." While Egyptian, Chaldean, Hindu, and other pagan religions do incorporate so-called "trinities," these have no resemblance to the Christian doctrine, which is unique and free from any heathen cultural vagaries. According to Christianity, the doctrine of the Trinity teaches that within the unity of the one Deity there are three separate Persons who are coequal in power, nature, and eternity. This teaching is derived from the clear teaching of Scripture beginning in the first chapter of the first book. In Genesis, at the dawn of creation, an interesting conversation took place:

"And God said, Let *us* make man in *our* image, after *our* likeness" (Genesis 1:26, emphasis added).

The significance of the plural *us* and *our* is no small issue. Either God was talking to Himself (a conjecture which even Jewish commentators reject), to the angels, or to other Persons, deliberately unidentified. That He would not have been talking to angels is clear because the next verse, referring to the creation of man, declares, "in the image of God created he him" (v. 27). God never created man in the image of angels, but in the *divine* image. In Genesis 1:26 the Father was addressing His Son and the Holy Spirit. No other explanation fits the context.

In Genesis 3:22, after Adam had sinned, God declared, "Man is become as one of *us*" (emphasis added); later, concerning the Tower of Babel, God said, "Let *us* go down and there confound their language" (Genesis 11:7, emphasis added). In both instances the mysterious plurality again emerges. Later the Old Testament prophets implied this same mysterious relationship within the Deity. In recounting his call to the prophetic office, Isaiah records that God asked, "Who will go for *us?*" (Isaiah 6:8, emphasis added). Why did not God say *me* instead of *us?* The answer is self-evident: God wished to testify of His threefold existence and nature.

In Zechariah, Jehovah spoke prophetically of the crucifixion and the second advent of the Messiah with these words: "I will pour upon the house of David, and upon the inhabitants of Jerusalem, the spirit of grace and of supplications: and they shall look upon me whom they have pierced, and they shall mourn for him, as one mourneth for *his only son,* and shall be in bitterness for him, as one that is in bitterness for *his* firstborn" (Zechariah 12:10).

Don't miss the importance of the *me* and *him*. Clearly the Lord God is speaking, yet He Himself changes the usage of *I* and *me* to *him,* and He speaks about being "pierced." There can be little room for question. God the Father is speaking of His beloved Son, the second Person of the Trinity, the One who shares the divine nature, the One who was to be made sin for us.

Quite often the question is asked, "How can God be one and yet three, or how can three added together produce one?" To understand this, we must realize that God is not tri-*plex* but tri-*une*. He is beyond the laws of finite mathematics. The word "one" itself has different meanings in the Old Testament. In Deuteronomy 6:4 Moses declared to Israel, "Hear, O Israel: The Lord our God is one Lord." Many persons seize upon this text as an allegedly "unanswerable" argument against the doctrine of the Trinity. They say, "Here the Bible says that God is one. If He is one, how can He also be three, or three in One?"

But what does the word "one" mean? Does it always indicate solitary existence? Genesis 2:24 recounts that God spoke of Adam and Eve becoming: "one flesh" *(bosor echod)*. God did not mean that Adam became Eve, or vice-versa; rather, He meant that in the marriage union the two persons became *as one* before Him. So we see that unity of a *composite* character was recognized by God Himself as existing within the world which He had created. The Lord Jesus Christ Himself recognized composite unity when He declared about people joined in marriage, "They are no more twain, but *one* flesh" (Mark 10:8, emphasis added).

Further use of the term "one" is found in Numbers 13:23,24, where the spies returning from the land of Canaan spoke of "one cluster of grapes" *(eschol echod)*, which could only mean that many grapes clung from *one* stem, although all drew their life from the same source. We can see, then, that the word "one" may refer to a composite unity rather than merely to a solitary "one."

If the United States should be attacked by a foreign power, everyone would "rise as one" to the defense of the country. Yet no one would say that everyone had instantaneously become "one person." Rather, we would be one in a *composite unity,* one in purpose or will to work toward a common goal. Scripture, however, indicates that the doctrine of the trinity of God is far above the idea of mere agreement of will or goal; it is a unity of the basic Scriptural nature of substance, and Deity is that substance (John 4:24; Hebrews 1:3). When we speak of being "one in faith and doctrine" or of "standing as one" in a time of crisis, we do not violate the sense of the word. Why then should we not accept composite unity where the nature of God is concerned? Certainly the Scriptures do not prohibit such a view.

The doctrine of the Trinity emerges from the New Testament Scriptures in several interesting places.

1. *The Incarnation.* The birth of the Lord Jesus Christ as described in the accounts in Matthew and Luke show that the

doctrine of the Trinity was not a later invention of theologians. Luke records, "The angel answered and said unto her, The *Holy Ghost* shall come upon thee, and the power of *the Highest* shall overshadow thee: therefore also that holy thing which shall be born of thee shall be called *the Son* of God" (Luke 1:35, emphasis added).

Since other passages of Scripture reveal that the term "Highest" refers to God the Father, we have in Luke a concrete instance of the Holy Spirit, the Father, and the Son all being mentioned together in the supernatural event of the Incarnation.

2. *The Baptism of Our Lord.* When Jesus Christ was baptized, the heavens opened and the *Holy Ghost* "descended in a bodily shape like a dove upon him, and a voice came from heaven, which said, Thou are my beloved Son; in thee *I am* well pleased" (Luke 3:21,22, emphasis added).

In these verses we see the Son being baptized, the Spirit descending upon Him, and the Father bearing testimony.

3. *Discourses of Christ.* In John 14 and 15 Christ is telling His disciples about the preeminency of the nature of God and the unity of triune composition. Jesus declared, "And *I* will pray *the Father*, and he shall give you another *Comforter*, that he may abide with you for ever; even *the Spirit* of truth; whom the world cannot receive, because it seeth him not, neither knoweth him: but ye know him; for he dwelleth with you, and shall be in you" (John 14:16,17, emphasis added). Our Lord here prays to the Father for the Spirit, and His awareness of triunity is quite apparent. In John 14:26 and 15:26 Christ uses the same formula, mentioning the three Persons of the Deity and indicating their unity, not only of purpose and will but of basic nature.

4. *Paul's Letters.* The Apostle Paul was definitely aware of the triune nature of God. He wrote, "The grace of the Lord Jesus Christ, and the love of God, and the communion of the Holy Ghost, be with you all. Amen" (2 Corinthians 13:14). It would have been difficult for Paul to give this benediction if the Father, Son, and Holy Spirit were not equal. Paul also describes Christ as "the fulness of the Deity bodily" (Colossians 2:9, literal translation) and as possessing God's very nature (Philippians 2:10; cf.

Isaiah 45:23).

5. *The Great Commission.* In Matthew 28:18-20 the Lord Jesus commissions the disciples to go out and preach the gospel and to make disciples of all people. He commands them also to baptize "in the name of the *Father,* and of the *Son,* and of the *Holy Ghost*" (emphasis added). Taken with the other passages bearing on the subject, this becomes an extremely powerful argument for the Christian doctrine of the Trinity.

6. *Creation.* Although the Bible does not explain to us how the three Persons are the one God, it tells us most emphatically that the Spirit of God created the world (Genesis 1:2), the Father created the world (Hebrews 1:2), and the Son created the world (Colossians 1:16). If you check the creation references in the New Testament, you will see that these particular references are bolstered by several others teaching the same things.

The Apostle Paul declared in Acts 17:24, "God that made the world and all things therein, seeing that he is Lord of heaven and earth, dwelleth not in temples made with hands." This forces us to an irresistible conclusion. As creation has been attributed to the Father, the Son, and the Holy Spirit singly and collectively, *they are the one God.* There cannot be three gods. The Scripture declares, "Look unto me, and be ye saved, all the ends of the earth: for I *am* God, and there is none else" (Isaiah 45:22). Hence there is unity in trinity and trinity in unity.

7. *The Resurrection of Christ.* A final instance of trinitarian emphasis is that of the Resurrection of our Lord. In John 2 Christ declared to the Jews, "Destroy this temple and in three days *I* will raise it up again" (v. 19, emphasis added). John hastens to tell us that Jesus was speaking of the Resurrection of His earthly body (v.21).

Other Scriptures state that Christ was raised by the agency of the Holy Spirit (Romans 8:11), and Peter states that the Father raised the Son (Acts 3:26), so that again God's Word affirms the triune existence.

Some, however, who believe in the personality of the Father and the Son, have doubts about the personality of the Holy Spirit. They need not remain in doubt. The Bible clearly indicates that the work which the Holy Spirit does can only be done by a Personality. For example, in John 16:13-15 the Spirit is called the Teacher sent by our Lord, who would lead us into all truth. It is further said that He would "reprove" the world. In Romans 8:27 He "intercedes" for the saints; in Ephesians 4:30 He may be "grieved"; in Acts 21 He commands and prophesies; and in Acts 5:3,4 Peter calls Him God. Certainly His claim to equality and personality is as real as that of the Father and Son.

We may not fully understand the great truth of the Trinity. However, we can see the rays of light which emanate from God's Word and which teach us that, in a mysterious sense beyond the comprehension of man's finite mind, God is *one* in nature but three in person and manifestation. Even as water, which may be converted into ice or steam, is one in nature though three in form, so also God is capable of being and doing what the mind of man cannot fathom. But in reverence man is still privileged to adore. It should be mentioned in passing that in the world of chemistry it is perfectly possible for a substance to exist simultaneously in three separate and distinct forms and yet remain basically one in structure or nature.

Water, for example, under pressure and in a vacuum at a given temperature below freezing exists simultaneously as both liquid, gas, and ice; yet it is identifiable always as water (H_2O), its basic nature. This is called in physics "the triple point of water" and is associated with the study of thermodynamics.

Those who cry "impossible" where the trinity of God or a similar event of the supernatural is concerned must compare its chemical counterpart in the natural world. Why can they not conceive of the Author of "the triple point" being supernaturally triune in His nature? If something is true of God's creation, can it not also be true of the Creator? If our Creator can design a "triple point of water," He can surely be a triune God Himself, and He can surely live within us and care about us.

The Scriptures assure us that this is so, and we accede to this teaching, for "he that cometh to God must believe that he is, and

that he is a rewarder of them that diligently seek him"
(Hebrews 11:6). From the Church Fathers, through the Reform-
ers, and on to the present day, historic Christianity continues to
echo the testimony of the prophets and the apostles of old. May
we profit from their insight and join with one voice of testimony
to that sublime revelation mirrored in the words of the majestic
hymn:

> Holy, Holy, Holy, Lord God Almighty,
> All thy works shall praise thy name in earth and
>   sky and sea.
> Holy, Holy, Holy, merciful and mighty,
> God in three Persons, blessed Trinity.

3

THE DEITY OF CHRIST

Colonel Robert Ingersoll, the famous agnostic, did much harm to the cause of Christianity with his skeptical propaganda. But buried in Ingersoll's lectures is evidence that he understood very well the nature of Christianity. In one of his lectures he stated:

"Christianity cannot live in peace with any other form of faith. If that religion be true, there is but one Savior, one inspired book and but one little narrow . . . path that leads to Heaven. Such a religion is necessarily uncompromising."

Much has changed since Ingersoll's era, but one factor remains — the denial of Christ as "God incarnate and the only Savior." Yet probably the most thoroughly documented teaching in the New Testament, except for that of the Resurrection, is that Jesus Christ was and always claimed to be God incarnate.

Hundreds of years before the birth of Christ, Isaiah declared that the Messiah was to be uniquely the Son of God and still in some mysterious sense God the Son. "For unto us a child is born, unto us a son is given: and the government shall be upon his shoulder: and his name shall be called Wonderful, Counsellor, mighty God, The everlasting Father, The Prince of Peace'' (Isaiah 9:6).

That this Person would share the nature of God Himself is further enunciated most clearly in the Gospel of John, sometimes called the Gospel of the deity of Christ.

John declares, "In the beginning was the Word, and the Word was with God, and the Word was God (1:1).'' In verse 14 John reveals that this same Word "became flesh and dwelt among us,'' and in verse 18 that "no one has seen God at any time; God, the only begotten, who is in the bosom of the Father, he has revealed him'' (literal translation).

The Greek word for "revealed" *(exsegesato)* literally means "lead out" or "make known.'' From the same word we derive our theological word "exegesis,'' literally "to take out.'' The Word was therefore made flesh for the express purpose of "exegeting'' or interpreting God the Father to mankind.

Many theologians have speculated concerning the Greek word *logos* (Word) in John 1:1. Some say it is a carryover from the Greek philosophy of Philo of Alexandria. Others maintain that it has a relationship to the Jewish Targum, which uses the Aramaic term *Memra* to express the divine nature.

Upon closer examination, the concept of the logos having come from Philo must be dismissed, for John was writing from the background of Judaism, and his illustration is from Oriental custom and *not* Greek philosophy.

In ancient days an oriental king held audience in his court within the throne room itself. Not wishing to be disturbed by the sight of some of his petitioning subjects, the king sometimes had a heavy curtain stretched across the back of the throne room, hiding the throne from the view of the petitioner. On the other side of the curtain stood the king's oracle or interpreter. On his right hand he wore the king's ring, and around his neck hung the medallion or royal seal symbolizing the authority to exercise judgment for the king. The oracle spoke for the king; he was known as his "interpreter" (Greek *logos*), the visible representative of the veiled monarch.

John uses this illustration to show us that even as the absolute authority to exercise judgment rested in the king's "interpreter" *(logos)* in the oriental courts, so the Lord Jesus, He who was "face to face with God" as the eternal Logos, became incarnate, taking upon Himself our form and as such becoming the mediator between God and man. He is the divine-human interpreter of the invisible God to fallen mankind.

The Lord Jesus carried with Him at all times the seal of His Father, performing all His miracles through the power of His Father (". . . the Father that dwelleth in me, he doeth the works" John 14:10; 5:30). As the ancient logos or interpreter in the oriental courts spoke in the name of the king behind the curtain, so the Man of Galilee perfectly interpreted or "exegeted" the will of His Father, who was veiled behind the curtain of eternity.

No wonder that it could be said by Christ, "He that hath seen me hath seen the Father" and "The Father loveth the Son, and hath given all things into his hand . . . that all men should honor the Son, even as they honor the Father" (John 14:9; 3:35; 5:23).

With this knowledge we can better understand the great majesty and authority which rested upon our Savior. The writer of the Epistle of the Hebrews described Christ's majesty as "the brightness of his glory and the express image of his person" (Hebrews 1:3). This passage, which literally reads, "The radiance or effulgence of His glory and the image imprinted by His nature or character," testifies again to the true identity of Jesus Christ. He is Deity stamped in human flesh for eternity.

The Pharisees objected to Christ because, among other things, He claimed true deity. In John 8:58 Christ unhesitatingly taught, "Before Abraham was, I am," and John stated that He made "himself equal with God" (John 5:18).

When we note that the identical terms used by Christ in John 8 are used by Jehovah in His discourse with Moses (Exodus 3:14ff.), we see that not only did Jesus fully understand His identity, but His enemies also understood His claim, for they "took up stones to stone Him" (John 8:59). The Jews stated clearly, "For a good work we stone thee not: but for blasphemy: and because that thou, being a man, makest thyself God" (John 10:33). This then was our Lord's claim—nothing short of eternal preexistence. Some persons wishing to reject this teaching point to John 9:9, where the term "I AM" also appears in the mouth of one who obviously was not Diety, thus "proving" that Christ's usage was not significant. They ignore, however, the context of John 8 and its companion texts, 18:5,6, when, after Christ declared that He was Jehovah (I AM), those who came to imprison Him fell to the ground until He permitted them to take Him. The context of John 8 and the Jews' taking up of stones to stone Him for blasphemy establishes Christ's claim positively.

Evidence of the deity of Christ abounds throughout the New Testament. The Apostle Paul speaks of the great "mystery of God, and of the Father, and of Christ" (Colossians 2:2) and states, "for in Him dwells all the fulness of the Deity bodily" (Colossians 2:9, literal translation). It is significant to note here that Paul does not use the term "Divinity" or "Divine quality" (*Theiotes*) but the word signifying absolute Deity (*Theotetos*), which differs from the former as essence differs from quality.

In Zechariah 12:10, as God is speaking, the terminology suddenly switches from the Father to the Son. "I will pour out my Spirit upon the house of David . . . and they shall look upon Me whom they have pierced, and they shall mourn for Him, as one mourneth for his only son." Note once again the triunity of God — "My Spirit . . . Me . . . Him."

When this is compared to Revelation 1:7, the application of Zechariah by the Holy Spirit is evident. "Behold, he cometh with clouds; and every eye shall see him, and they also which pierced him: and all kindreds of the earth shall wail because of him."

The deity of our Lord fairly leaps from countless pages of the New Testament which deal with the mysterious relationship between Christ and His Father. This relationship caused the Apostle Paul to exult, "Looking for that blessed hope and the appearing of the glory of the great God and of our Savior, Jesus Christ" (Titus 2:13, literal translation). "The great God" is the antecedent of the phrase "our Savior Jesus Christ." It is this same "great God" who could dogmatically say to His antagonists, "If ye believe not that I AM, ye shall die in your sins" (John 8:24).

Link upon link the golden chain of the deity of Christ is forged through the pages of Scripture until at last it rests complete about the neck of Him who by angelic proclamation is declared to be "King of Kings and Lord of Lords" (1 Timothy 6:15), a chain which clasps together at the royal medallion of the Lion of the tribe of Judah (Revelation 5:5).

It is little wonder, then, that through the ages men have been willing to "face the tyrant's brandished steel and the lions' gory mane" and to face the fires of a thousand deaths for the love of Him who is conqueror of death, because He and He alone is "Prince of Life" (Acts 3:15).

The Christ of Scripture is not the wishy-washy bloodless Jesus of certain liberal theologians, nor is He "the divine principle or Christ-idea" of Christian Science, Unity, or the other gnostic cults. He is not the angelic creature of Jehovah's Witnesses, the "advanced medium" of the Spiritualists, or the abstract Principle of philosophic speculation. He is most certainly not the "historical Jesus" gouged out of the New Testament by either ignoring or minimizing sections of the divine Record.

The Christ of Scripture is the very Oracle of God Himself, designated Logos or spokesman for the Father, in whose nail-pierced hands the fate of all creation rests. Truly God has spoken unto us in this age "by his Son, whom he hath appointed heir of all things, by whom also he made the worlds" (Hebrews 1:2).

It is no wonder, then, that Paul could write: "Wherefore God also hath highly exalted him, and given him a name which is above every name: that at the name of Jesus every knee should bow, of things in heaven, and things in earth, and things under the earth; and that every tongue should confess that Jesus Christ is Lord, to the glory of God the Father'' (Philippians 2:9-11).

Few persons who read this quotation from the Word of God fully realize that it is a direct testimony of the deity of Jesus Christ. Philippians 2:10 is a paraphrase of Isaiah 45:23 in the Greek or Septuagint version, which was in use at the time of our Savior. Paul therefore cites Isaiah 45:23, where Jehovah is speaking, and applies it to the Lord Jesus Christ as positive proof of the mysterious union between God the Father and God the Son.

By virtue of His true deity and perfect humanity, Christ transcends all human personalities. Muhammad, it is claimed, was a prophet; Buddha, a teacher; Confucius, an ethical politician; Zoroaster, a sage; Ghandi, a Hindu mystic and social reformer. Though the teachings of these dead men still live, their bones lie mouldering in the graveyards of earth. But the Christ of Scripture not only lives in His teachings and in the hearts of those who trust Him, but He lives "at the right hand of the majesty on high" and makes intercession for us with the Father (Hebrews 7:25).

Christianity, then, does not rest entirely upon the principles, ethics, and teachings of Jesus, but upon the facts of the Incarnation and the Resurrection, the fact that the eternal Word truly became flesh and dwelt among us, and that we truly beheld His glory, "the glory as of the unique Son of the Father, full of grace and truth" (John 1:14, literal translation).

We can believe in nothing less than a divine-human Redeemer, for Scripture knows none other.

THE LAST ADAM

At this point, though it need not occupy a great deal of our time, it is important to note some facts about our Lord's human nature, lest we have·an incomplete picture of His whole being and Incarnation.

In Jesus Christ, God became man in a unique but very real sense. Scripture tells us that in Him (Christ) "all the fulness of the Deity resided in the flesh" (Colossians 2:9, literal translation). But although He never ceased possessing His divine nature, Christ accepted the limitations of human life with one important exception—He knew no sin. Jesus Christ alone could say, "The prince of this world cometh, and hath nothing in me," for He alone was "holy, harmless, undefiled, separate from sinners" (John 14:30; Hebrews 7:26).

He is designated in Scripture as the "last Adam" and "the Lord from heaven" (1 Corinthians 15:45-47). His was the zenith of human nature as the Father always intended it to be.

However, granting the truth of all this, we must not fall into the error of some fundamentalist theologians who have emphasized Christ's deity at the expense of His humanity, thus making Him God without a corresponding acknowledgment of His self-limited humanity. We must also avoid the excesses of liberal theologians, who have emphasized His humanity to the detriment of His deity. The "sane center," theologically speaking, must be the recognition of both of our Lord's natures in their proper context and in the perspective of all that the Scriptures teach concerning the Savior.

Let us never forget that the limitations of our Lord's earthly life do not detract from either His deity or His humanity. Some of Christ's self-imposed limitation (Philippians 2:8-11) can be seen clearly in Scripture and should be recognized as the logical outgrowth of the Incarnation. Limitation, then, should never be interpreted as either weakness or imperfection.

The New Testament irrefutably teaches that Christ did not exercise at least three prime attributes of deity while on the earth prior to His Resurrection. These were omniscience, omnipotence, and omnipresence. Had He done so while a man He could not have been perfect humanity.

Our Lord deliberately limited Himself as a man in order to be truly human. Thus it could be said of Him that He "increased in wisdom and stature, and in favor with God and man" (Luke 2:52). On one occasion, when asked for the day and the hour of His second coming to earth, the Master plainly said He did not know. He then went on to state that such knowledge was in the possession of the Father, to whom He always deferred (Matthew 24:36).

The miracles of our Lord offer further proof of His limitations as a man, for He did not hesitate to teach that He personally worked none of them, and that it was the Father who performed the works (John 5:19, 30; John 8:28; 10:32; 10:37, 38; 14:10).

We do not shrink from the Scriptural truth that during His earthly life the Son of Man was inferior in rank to His Father, for He Himself taught, "The Father is greater that I" (John 14:28). Yet, while such inferior position as a man existed, in His divine nature He was always the Father's equal (John 5:18).

It can be said on good Biblical ground that all of Christ's miracles, powers, and supernatural information were the result of the Father's action through Him, thus safeguarding our Lord's identity as a true man (John 14:10; John 5:30). Let us never forget, though, that the Father was Christ's personal Tutor and intimate Companion, and that all the knowledge He did possess was perfect knowledge, for from perfection only perfection can come (John 8:28; John 12:47-50). The late Dr. Donald Grey Barnhouse once said that "Jesus might not have known that 12 x 12 was 144, but He would never have taught that it was 145." Christ's perfect humanity as the last Adam would automatically have precluded such an error or, for that matter, any error, even to the identification of the true authors of Biblical books, such as Moses, Isaiah, Daniel, etc.

It is wise, then, to keep both of our Lord's natures in their proper relationships with each other in Scripture, for it is just as much heresy to say that Jesus is only God as it is to say that Jesus is only Man. If Jesus is only God, His humanity is a hollow sham;

He is not truly human and "cannot be touched with the feeling of our infirmities" (Hebrews 4:15; Matthew 8:17).

On the other hand, if Jesus were only man, even if a superior man among men, then the Messiah of Hebrew prophecy becomes a religious myth, the incarnation of legend; God does not have a Son at all; and the Babe of Bethlehem's manger was not "God with us" (Isaiah 9:6; Matthew 1:23).

These are the two extremes that must be avoided at all costs. Christ is neither all God nor all man but is instead the *God-Man* of divine prediction, the true Savior of the world.

Jesus Christ, then, is God the Son, the second Person of the Trinity, the One who loved us and died that we might live forever in the everlasting fellowship of the redeemed.

Far from being a myth, Christ's historical existence is better validated than that of all the prophets combined. It was said of Helen of Troy that she possessed the face that launched a thousand ships, but it can be said of Jesus Christ alone that He provided the inspiration, love, and devotion that launched a billion souls from darkness to eternal light.

Here is hope for the hopeless soul, power for the powerless sinner, and victory for the defeated life. All this is true because of who Christ is, and because He alone of the sons of men "hath abolished death, and hath brought life and immortality to light through the gospel" (2 Timothy 1:10). We can joyfully join in the confession with Thomas of old, "My Lord and my God," for as Christ Himself stated, "You call me Lord and Master, and so I AM" (John 13:13).

4

THE VIRGIN BIRTH OF CHRIST

A prominent advertisement in a leading Philadelphia newspaper caught my attention in the preparation of this chapter. It read, "Want to hear a controversial young preacher? Sunday at 11:10 A.M. *Time* magazine wrote up his denunciation of hell. He's against capital punishment! Doesn't believe in the virgin birth. . . ."

We might have guessed that the clock had been turned back 50 years, when such advertisements were common. But here was a recognized, contemporary minister denying the historic position of his own church — the church that had ordained him to the ministry!

In the letters-to-the-editor column of a large Christian periodical, another young minister supported this clergyman in his denial of the virgin birth and then dissented from the vicarious atonement and the bodily Resurrection of Christ for good measure. He is still in good standing with his own church; in fact, he was promoted to a higher position despite his published views!

Far from being a dead issue, the doctrine of the virgin birth of our Lord continues to provide theologians with an area of intense interest because in a very real sense it is the pivot upon which the fact of the Incarnation itself rests.

In the great controversy of the twenties and thirties between liberalism and fundamentalism, the virgin birth of Christ became a veritable rallying cry for conservative Christians. These responsible leaders saw in the liberal denials of this Biblical truth a direct attack not only upon the authority of the Scriptures but upon the very character of Christ as well.

In his magnum opus, *The Virgin Birth of Christ*, the late Dr. J. G. Machen with scholarly precision dissected the various objections to the Biblical teaching and thoroughly refuted those who attempted to teach that the virgin birth was merely an appendage of paganism carried over into Christianity, a later theological device of zealous but misled Christians to add further glory to the character of Jesus.

We are primarily concerned in our study, however, with the evidence offered from Scripture and its contemporary relevance for Christians. For if the Bible really does teach the virgin birth of Christ as a historical event, and if it can be shown that both the Jews and our Lord recognized its importance, then to any person who regards the Bible as prima facie evidence the virgin birth must be regarded as an integral part of Christian theology.

The doctrine of the virgin birth of Christ is indissolubly joined with Old Testament prophecy. The words of Isaiah the prophet bear eloquent testimony to a certain mysterious double event:

> Therefore the Lord himself shall give you a sign; Behold, a virgin shall conceive, and bear a son, and shall call his name Immanuel. Butter and honey shall he eat, that he may know to refuse the evil, and choose the good. For before the child shall know to refuse the evil, and choose the good, the land that thou abhorrest shall be forsaken of both her kings (Isaiah 7:14-16).

On the universal or futuristic side, the prophecy refers to the Incarnation of the Lord Jesus Christ, a fact substantiated by Matthew's reference to it: ''Behold a virgin shall be with child, and shall bring forth a son, and they shall call his name Immanuel, which being interpreted is, God with us'' (Matthew 1:23).

Matthew uses the unqualified term for virgin, *parthenos* (the Greek equivalent of the Hebrew *bethula*, "absolute virgin"), thereby establishing beyond doubt that Mary was an undefiled maiden.

Isaiah further tells us that the child would be a divine child: "His name shall be called Wonderful, Counsellor, The mighty God, The everlasting Father, The Prince of Peace." The child would reign forever, and "the zeal of the Lord of hosts will perform this" (Isaiah 9:6,7).

Micah the prophet revealed that this child would be born in Bethlehem, the City of David, in keeping with Isaiah's prophecy that He would be the Son of David (Micah 5:2; cf. Isaiah 9:7).

Furthermore, the prophets predicted that this babe of Bethlehem's manger would one day become the Messiah of Calvary's Cross, the Savior who would be "cut off" or crucified for the sins of the "whole world" (Isaiah 53; Daniel 9:26; 1 John 2:2).

They also declared that this same child would rise again to life and would come in the power of Almighty God with His holy angels to sift the sons of men with eternal judgment (Zechariah 12:10; cf. Revelation 1:7-9). All these prophecies were fulfilled to the letter by Jesus Christ of Nazareth, and they only remain to be consummated at His triumphant return as Judge of the world (1 Thessalonians 4:13-17; cf. Hebrews 9:28).

Both Matthew and Luke declare that the human fulfillment of God's plan as the Christchild was conceived in Mary (Matthew 1:18-25; Luke 1:30-38). Our Lord, it is revealed, was conceived in the virgin's womb by a direct act of the Holy Spirit, wholly apart from human agency. The record speaks eloquently for itself:

> Now the birth of Jesus Christ was on this wise: when as his mother Mary was espoused to Joseph, before they came together, she was found

with child of the Holy Ghost. Then Joseph her husband, being a just man, and not willing to make her a public example, was minded to put her away privily. But while he thought on these things, behold, the angel of the Lord appeared unto him in a dream, saying, Joseph, thou son of David, fear not to take unto thee Mary thy wife: for that which is conceived in her is of the Holy Ghost. And she shall bring forth a son, and thou shalt call his name JESUS: for he shall save his people from their sins. Now all this was done that it might be fulfilled which was spoken of the Lord by the prophet, saying, Behold, a virgin shall be with child, and shall bring forth a son, and they shall call his name Immanuel, which being interpreted is, God with us (Matthew 1:18-23).

Two very clear facts emerge: (1) Mary's conception was "*before* they came together"; and (2) Joseph, acting precisely as a man would be expected to react under such circumstances, was dissuaded from "putting her away privily" only by divine intervention, by announcement that the virgin birth was to be a fulfillment of inspired prophecy.

Added to this record is the strong internal evidence of an interesting discourse between Christ and His Jewish antagonists. In the heat of argument the Jews appeared to imply that Christ was an illegitimate child. This accusation would have been meaningless unless the *fact* of the virgin birth or at least its claim were known to them and to our Lord. This conversation, as recorded by John, is most revealing.

I know that ye are Abraham's seed; but ye seek to kill me, because my word hath no place in you. I speak that which I have seen with my Father: and ye do that which ye have seen with your father. They answered and said unto him, Abraham is our father. Jesus saith unto them, If ye were Abraham's children, ye would do the works of Abraham . . . . Then said they to him, We be not born of *fornication;* we have one Father, even God.* Jesus said unto them, If God were your Father, ye would love me: for I proceeded forth and came from God; neither came I of myself, but he sent me (John 8:37-39,41,42, emphasis added).

The Jewish accusation of illegitimacy evoked from our Lord one of the most blistering denunciations of His Pharisaical critics contained in Scripture.

---

*The context admits to a dual interpretation here, the other meaning being that the Jews were merely affirming their covenant promises. I think it is a possibility but the other interpretation is just as likely.

Why do ye not understand my speech? Even because ye cannot hear my word. Ye are of your father the devil, and the lusts of your father ye will do. He was a murderer from the beginning, and abode not in the truth, because there is no truth in him. When he speaketh a lie, he speaketh of his own: for he is a liar, and the father of it. And because I tell you the truth, ye believe me not. Which of you convinceth me of sin? And if I say the truth, why do ye not believe me? *He that is of God heareth God's words: ye therefore hear them not, because ye are not of God.* Then answered the Jews, and said unto him, Say we not well that thou are a Samaritan and hast a devil? Jesus answered, I have not a devil but I honor my Father, and *ye do dishonor me* (John 8:43-49, emphasis added).

In these passages Christ established the fact that God was His Father, *not* Joseph, and that Satan rather than God was the spiritual father of His antagonists. In addition, He specifically established the explicit fact that he was not "born of fornication" but was of unique divine paternity.

Clearly, then, the virgin birth, according to Scripture, was the instrument utilized by God to bring about the Incarnation. The biological fact of the virgin birth in itself should never constitute a barrier to faith and acceptance.

The fact is, however, that those who deny the virgin birth are really denying the authority of the Gospel writers on rationalistic grounds. While human reason is certainly important, Scripture indicates that in the Adamic fall every area of man's physical, mental, and spiritual capacities were impaired. So reason, though useful, is by no means a safe criterion for determining the validity of divine truth. The angel's reference to Isaiah 7 places a divine imprimatur, one might say, upon both the Old Testament prophecy and its New Testament fulfillment. It is therefore difficult to read Matthew, Luke, and especially John without concluding that the Incarnation is indissolubly connected to the virgin birth.

If we accept the God who could form the universe, open the Red Sea, deliver Elijah on Carmel, and preserve Daniel in the lion's den, then we should be able to accept the miracle of His Son's virgin birth. If we believe that Adam, the first of the human family, was created without benefit of parents, certainly the birth of the "last Adam" (1 Corinthians 15:45) should provide no obstacle to a mature faith.

Some critics would ask, "Could not God have created Christ sinless apart from the virgin birth?"* Now we know that with God all things are possible, but this is not the question before us. The question is, "What does the divine record reveal to us regarding the instrument or vehicle of the Incarnation?" Our Lord Himself affirmed His own sinlessness in unmistakable terms (John 8:46), and Scripture *links this sinlessness with the virgin birth,* identifying the virgin birth itself as the precise channel of that incarnate act.

Those who deny the virgin birth would do well to recall our Lord's intense displeasure at being called illegitimate (John 8:41-47). And if Joseph or any other mortal were his father, then according to Scripture the charge would have been true (Matthew 1:18)! But both Matthew and Luke vigorously rule out any such concept. By challenging the integrity of the Gospel narratives of the virgin birth, those who would retain a so-called "rational view of Scripture" are in danger of questioning the integrity of God Himself. Paradoxically enough, although these same people maintain that God inspired the Gospels, they refuse to accept what the record so plainly states.

The positive teaching of Scripture, however, is clear. Through the lineage of David and in David's city, in the womb of a virgin whom God had prepared, the eternal Word was made flesh (John 1:1, 14) and emerged in the world of men to be rejected by His own people but to purchase eternal redemption for those who would believe in Him. The true significance of the virgin birth of Christ is not so much the miraculous element of God intervening and suspending the laws of nature, but the fact

---

*Some Christians are led into the fallacy that unless Christ was virgin-born He could not have been sinless. Such a view would limit the omnipotence of God, "for with God all things are possible." The answer, of course, is not that God was limited to the virgin birth to actuate the Incarnation but that He decreed that the virgin birth would be the *means* of its realization.

that God chose to become man in Jesus Christ, "Who for us men and our salvation was incarnate of the Holy Ghost and born of the virgin Mary." The prophecies of the Old Testament, hoary with age, burn brightly once again in the manger of Bethlehem. The testimony of Peter at Pentecost, "thy holy child Jesus" (Acts 4:27), also flares out with new meaning. God was manifest in the flesh and born of a virgin!

The doctrines of the authority of the Scriptures and the virgin birth are therefore inseparably joined. The Christian church has always held that they are both necessary to the unity of the whole.

It is paradoxical indeed to affirm the cardinal doctrines of Scripture and yet to deny Scripture itself! Such unbiblical speculations "unsettle the faith of many" and impugn the record that God has given of His Son (1 John 5:9). In a very real sense such a view indicts God for perjury (1 John 5:10).

In view of all these facts, the virgin birth is, first of all, an important Biblical teaching. It is not to be treated lightly. It is to be believed by all who accept the Scriptures as authoritative.

Secondly, it is a definite sin to disbelieve or question this teaching, because it is so closely related to the Incarnation of our Lord Himself. On this issue Dr. J. G. Machen wisely sums up our thinking.

What then is our conclusion? Is belief in the virgin birth necessary to every man if he is to be a believer in the Lord Jesus Christ? The question is wrongly put when it is put in that way. Who can tell exactly how much knowledge of the facts about Christ is necessary if a man is to have saving faith? None but God can tell. Some knowledge is certainly required, but how much is required we cannot say. "Lord, I believe; help thou mine unbelief" said a man in the Gospel who was saved. Though today there are many men of little faith, many who are troubled by the voices that are heard on all sides . . . What right have we to say that full knowledge and full conviction are necessary before a man can put his trust in the crucified and risen Lord? What right have we to say that no man can be saved before he has come to a full conviction regarding the stupendous miracle narrated in the first chapters of Matthew and Luke? . . .

One thing at least is clear: even if the belief in the virgin birth is not necessary to every Christian, it is necessary to Christianity. And it is necessary to the corporate witness of the Church. . . .

Let it never be forgotten that the virgin birth is an integral part of the New Testament witness about Christ, and that that witness is strongest when it is taken as it stands. . . .[1]

There is little to be added to Dr. Machen's analysis except to say that the virgin birth is not peripheral and that we cannot logically, rationally, or theologically divorce it from the Incarnation. God did become man in Jesus Christ — this is the crucial truth — but He did it through the miracle of the virgin birth. Anything less than this is fundamentally unsound and spiritually damaging to any system of theology that purports to be Christian.

CHAPTER NOTE

1. J. Gresham Machen, *The Virgin Birth of Christ* (Grand Rapids: Baker Book House, 1930), pp. 395-396.

5

CHRIST DIED FOR US

Why did Christ die? A simple question? Yes, but the answer is most profound.

We might answer, as a Christian, "Christ died for me," but exactly what does this mean? Did He die merely to appease God's wrath against us? Did He die only as an example for us? Exactly why did Jesus die? What does the atonement really mean? The understanding of this basic Scriptural truth eludes many, but it is vital to the soul's redemption and to our spiritual growth.

To understand this doctrine we must go back to the Old Testament and its sacrificial offerings.

The blood of animals, in itself, was never efficacious to cleanse from sin (Hebrews 10:4). Rather, the blood symbolized the element of life offered for the life of the sinner. God always intended that the entire system of sacrificial offerings be of expiatory significance (Job 1:5; 42:3,9; Leviticus 17:2-11). The alienation of man from God through human sin made necessary a reconciliation, and the form of that reconciliation was ordained to be a cross.

The Jewish sacrificial system with its "covering" offerings (the Hebrew word for atonement, *kaphir*, means "covering") made possible man's approach to the presence of a holy God. The sprinkling of blood upon the mercy seat in the tabernacle (Leviticus 16:15,16) and the sprinkling of the blood of the passover lamb (Exodus 12:7) underscored the importance of substitutionary sacrifice under the Old Covenant made between Jehovah and Israel. In the New Testament, and particularly in the Book of Hebrews, the significance of such sacrifices is revealed in the Lord Jesus Christ, who is pictured as both officiating Priest and atoning Sacrifice (Hebrews 9:11-15; 10:10-12).

Isaiah 53 remains the classic appeal for the doctrine of the vicarious atonement: "Surely he hath borne our griefs, and carried our sorrows. . . . He *was* wounded for our transgressions, he *was* bruised for our iniquities: the chastisement of our peace *was* upon him; and with his stripes we are healed. All we like sheep have gone astray; we have turned everyone to his own way; and the Lord hath laid on him the iniquity of us all" (Isaiah 53:4-6).

Particularly significant in these verses is the fact that Christ's life was made "an offering for sin" (Isaiah 53:10). Isaiah stresses repeatedly the vicarious aspects of the Messianic offering when he states "for the transgression of my people was he stricken. . . . He shall bear their iniquities. . . . He bare the sin of many" (Isaiah 53:8,11,12). The word "vicarious" comes from the Latin *vicar*, which literally means "in place of" or "a substitute." Daniel the prophet further reminds us that in the prophetic plan of God "shall Messiah be cut off, but not for himself" (Daniel 9:26). Certainly, the vicarious atonement of the Messiah of Israel forms one of the great pillars upon which rests the entire structure of the Judeo-Christian religions. The Old Testament points like a massive arrow to the consummation of all sacrifices, an event of immeasurable importance and worth.

In the New Testament, John the Baptist declares, "Behold the Lamb of God, which taketh away the sin of the world" (John 1:29), and our Savior Himself declares His flesh and blood to be the sin offering for the whole world (John 6:51). When coupled with Paul's declaration "the church of God which he hath purchased with his own blood" (Acts 20:28), such statements give an incontrovertible answer to the question "Why did Jesus die?"

But there is still another question that demands an answer. *"For whom* did Christ die?" One leading school of thought has always maintained that Christ died and shed His blood *only* for those whom God chose to be redeemed. This view, commonly known as Calvin's "limited atonement," has many supporters. However, John the Apostle tells us that Christ gave His life as a propitiation for our sin (i.e., the elect), though not for ours *only* but for the sins of the *whole world* (1 John 2:2). Some may quibble about passages which emphasize the term "all," even attempting to make it a restrictive term, but they cannot evade John's usage of "whole" (Greek *holos*). In the same context the apostle quite cogently points out that "the whole *(holos)* world lies in wickedness" or, more properly, "in the lap of the wicked one" (1 John 5:19, literal translation). If we assume that "whole" applies only to the chosen or elect of God, then the "whole" world does not "lie in the lap of the wicked one." This, of course, all reject.

It is sometimes argued that Christ's blood was *sufficient* for the sins of the whole world but *efficient* only for those who accept Him. However, the question concerns not the sufficiency or efficiency of the sacrifice but the identity of those for whom it was offered. Semantics may be good for intellectual gymnastics but they are a poor substitute for revelation.

Others attempt to undercut the substitutionary aspects of the atonement by pointing out that while Christ died vicariously, His death was not substitutionary. This they accomplish by redefining the meaning of the word vicarious, so that for them vicarious becomes "one death for the benefit of all," but not literally *in place of each.*

Such thinkers point out that the Greek preposition *huper*, often translated "for" in the New Testament, has, in certain atonement contexts, two separate meanings. It may mean "benefit" *or* "substitution." They point to such passages as John 15:13, 1 Timothy 2:5,6, and 1 Peter 3:18, and particularly those selected passages where the preposition *anti* (which they agree is the stronger of the two words), translated "for," appears.

If *anti* were used, they say, instead of *huper*, the "absolute certainty" of the idea of substitution could never be successfully challenged. They reject, however, a very important aspect of grammar at this point, and we must clarify the issue for all to see.

Let us consider the facts. In speaking of His substitutionary sacrifice, Christ declared, "The Son of Man . . . came to give his life a ransom for *[anti]* many" (Matthew 20:28, emphasis added). At the Last Supper, during which Christ emphasized the vicarious nature of Calvary, He said, "This is my body which is given for *[anti]* you" (Luke 22:19, emphasis added). The usage of *anti* in such passages as Matthew 5:38, ("An eye *for* an eye"), Luke 11:11 ("will he *for* a fish give him a serpent?"), and Matthew 2:22 ("Archelaeus reigned *in the place of [anti]* his father Herod") reveals unmistakably that substitution is the indisputable theme and meaning of Christ's death.

Consequently, *anti* as well as *huper* is used to refer to the vicarious nature of Christ's atonement. Since the meaning of *huper* must be determined by its context, the two terms are virtually interchangeable in context.

To illustrate this, let us take Paul's statement in 2 Corinthians 5:20,21: "Now then we are ambassadors for Christ, as though God did beseech you by us; we pray *you* in Christ's stead *[huper]*, be ye reconciled to God. For he hath made him *to be* sin *for [huperemon]* us, who knew no sin." This alone establishes the interchangeability of *huper* with *anti*. Another instance is Philemon 13, "Whom I would have retained with me, that *in thy stead [huper]* he might have ministered unto me." That *huper* in these instances means "in place of" is undeniable.

Another statement of the Apostle Paul, "The love of Christ constraineth us; because we thus judge, that if one died *for [huper]* all, then were all dead" (2 Corinthians 5:14), unquestionably connotes substitutiòn. It would be ridiculous to believe that *huper* would here mean only "benefit," since such a rendering would destroy the significance of the passage.

Dr. William G. T. Shedd has summed all this up with a characteristically brilliant paragraph:

> The word "for" of the Greek words *anti, huper, dia,* and *peri,* of which it is the translation admitting of different senses, may of course be differently applied according to the nature of the subject, and yet the doctrine remains unchanged. As it might be proper to say that Christ suffered *instead* of us, although it would be absurd to say that He suffered *instead* of our offences, it is sufficient if the different applications of the word carry a consistent meaning. To die *instead of* us and to die *on account of* our offences perfectly agree. But this change of the expression necessarily arises from the change of the subject ... for although dying *for* our benefit is perfectly intelligible, dying *for the benefit* of our offences is no less absurd than dying *instead of* our offences. In the light of these facts it is easy to see why the New Testament writers employ *huper* so often rather than *anti* to denote the relation of Christ's death to man's salvation. The latter preposition excludes the idea of benefit or advantage and specifies only the idea of substitution. The former may include *both* ideas. Whenever, therefore, the sacred writer would express *both* together and at *once*, he selects the preposition *huper*. In so doing, he teaches both that Christ died *in* the sinner's place and *for* the sinner's benefit.

The Epistle to the Hebrews reminds us that the Lord Jesus tasted "death for every man" (Hebrews 2:9), and in his Epistle to the Ephesians Paul, following the typology of the Old Testament, states, Christ "hath given *for* us [as] an offering and a sacrifice to God" (5:2). Peter tells us that "who his own self bare our sins in his own body on the tree" (1 Peter 2:24). The word for "bare" *(anaphero)* in context here carries the thought "to bear sins upon the Cross in order to expiate them by suffering death," and beyond question it denotes vicarious sacrifice.

Throughout church history theologians have tried to explain the ramifications of our Lord's sacrifice. As a result, various "theories" were developed. Although the heart of the atonement is its vicarious (substitutionary) nature, other aspects of it may enlarge upon its relationship to the entire plan of God. It is not wrong to theorize. Error arises only when speculation and theorizing run contrary to the expressed declaration of Scripture.

The various theories of the atonement (ransom to Satan, recapitulation, satisfaction, moral influence, example, governmental, penal, mystical, etc.) make definite contributions to the idea of atonement but by themselves they do not deal with the basic issue of man's alienation from God and the necessity of vicarious reconciliation.

THE RANSOM THEORY

The ransom theory maintains that Christ's death was a ransom paid to Satan in order to "cancel the just claims which the latter had on man." Origen, the great early church theologian, propounded this concept, relying upon such passages as Matthew 20:28, 1 Timothy 2:6, and Galatians 3:13.

The difficulty with Origen's concept is that Satan has no claim upon the soul of man; Christ's death as a "ransom" (1 Peter 1:18) paid fully the price for the transgression of the holy law of God. It was *God* who was offended by man's transgression, not Satan. True, a definite "ransom" or redemption price was necessary for the human race, but Scripture tells us that it was a redemption from the power of sin.

If the Scripture teaches us anything, it teaches us beyond question that the Lord Jesus Christ is the propitiation of *all* our sins (Hebrews 10:10). God's righteousness is established through His judgment of sin and His satisfaction of this antipathy by the death of Jesus Christ. Thus God is able to forgive unregenerate men and yet continue to maintain His own righteousness.

THE RECAPITULATION THEORY

Irenaeus, another of the early church theologians, propounded the "recapitulation theory," stating that Christ's death "satisfied" God's justice. Dr. James Orr has expressed it, "that Christ recapitulates in himself all the stages of human life, including those which belong to our state as sinners." The difficulty with Irenaeus' concept is that it emphasizes a vicarious *life* as well as a vicarious death.

About vicarious death Scripture leaves no doubt. However, there is little, if any, evidence that Christ lived a vicarious life on our behalf. Rather, the Scripture teaches us that God imputes to us the righteousness of Christ, though there is a singular absence of any vicarious relation to His human life. This so-called recapitualtion theory of Iranaeus was very popular in the early Christian church but was eventually replaced by the satisfaction theory of Anselm.

THE SATISFACTION THEORY

Anselm maintained that God's righteousness could be appeased in only two ways: either by punishment or by satisfaction. God, according to Anselm, chose satisfaction instead of punishment. By perfectly obeying the law of God, our Lord need not have died under the curse of sin. But since He did choose to die for the race, the reward or benefit of His sacrifice became the property of penitent sinners, and God's honor and righteousness were satisfied. Anselm's theory was no doubt a step in the right direction. However, he almost completely overlooked the *penalty of sin*, which is death (Romans 6:23), and the fact that Christ died as a *penalty* for the sins of mankind and not merely, as Dr. Louis Berkhof puts it, "as a tribute offered to the honor of the Father."

Anselm left the door open for a penance system to be added to the work of Christ, as the Roman Catholic Church has done. Berkhof states, "In Anselm's representation there is merely an external transfer of the merits of Christ to man. It contains no indication of the way in which the work of Christ for man is communicated to man. There is no hint of the mystical union of Christ and believers, nor of faith, or accepting the righteousness of Christ. Since the whole transaction appears to be rather commercial, the theory is often called the 'commercial theory.' "

THE MORAL IINFLUENCE THEORY

Another prominent theory is the moral influence theory. According to this view, Christ's death revealed the love of God for the fallen race, but the influence of the moral character of God as revealed in the sacrifice of Christ acts upon the hearts of men in such a way as to bring the sinner to a recognition of his own failure and the necessity of trusting Christ.

Not only does this theory rule out vicarious atonement, but it also rejects altogether the penal concept of Christ dying to pay the penalty for human transgressions. It assumes that the human will is capable of response to the moral influence of God despite the curse of sin. Scripture, however, points out that man is "dead in . . . sins" (Colossians 2:13) and that it is only the energizing of the Holy Spirit through grace which makes possible the volitional act of an individual whereby he comes into a saving relationship with the Lord Jesus Christ (Ephesians 2:1). Certainly a moral influence is exerted by our Savior's sacrifice, but it alone does not do away with the necessity of perfect reconciliation through the blood of the Cross (Romans 5:10; Colossians 1:21).

The moral influence theory leads to great subjectivism. The effects of Adam's sin upon the human race can never be minimized. In the Fall every property of man's physical, moral, and spiritual being suffered the effects of the Adamic transgression. To assume that fallen man is capable of being successfully influenced apart from the grace of God is patently antibiblical.

THE EXAMPLE THEORY

Linked with the moral influence theory, the example theory teaches that God is not so much concerned with punishing sin as He is with finding obedience in the lives of men. While partially true, this theory denies the moral depravity of the human soul and maintains that Christ's death was exemplary, not vicarious or penal. It teaches that by obedience to Christ's perfect example of selfless love, man may find his peace with God. This particular theory grew out of the Unitarian heresy propounded by Faustus Socinus in the sixteenth century. While containing an element of truth, it is basically fallacious. The example theory pictures our Lord as no more than a perfect human being who set a perfect example. But since no one has ever been able to perfectly follow His example, how can we benefit from such a view of His death?

While none of the theories of the atonement is complete in itself, each contains some truth. Certainly Christ's death was a ransom for the sins of the whole world (1 Timothy 2:6), and certainly it was an act of reconciliation on God's part (2 Corinthians 5:18,19; Colossians 2:13). We do not hesitate to affirm that the atonement exerts a great moral influence over man, though not an influence sufficient to overcome the moral degeneration of the Adamic judgment. Although Christ is an example for us to follow, His death involves far more than exemplary love and obedience. The death of our Lord entails more than all man's theories can grasp. To understand the atonement of the Lord Jesus Christ, one must come to view the holiness of God and the "exceeding sinfulness of sin" in the radiant light of divine revelation. Only as we understand the fact that no *one* aspect of the atonement fully explains the character of the *whole* will we come to appreciate the marvelous display of boundless grace which was offered to a fallen race by the mercy of a loving Creator.

One thing is clear, however. The atonement is far more than a shallow "at-one-ment" (a popular perversion of the translation of the Greek *katalagge*—"to reconcile"). Rather, it is a sublime declaration of the fact that God's justice demands perfect satisfaction and that this was accomplished once for all when God "made him *to be* sin for us, who knew no sin" (2 Corinthians 5:21) and we were "reconciled to God by the death of his Son" (Romans 5:10).

The Apostle Paul traces the grand design of our redemption in 1 Corinthians 15, where in his capsule definition of the gospel he begins by stating first that "Christ died *for* our sins" (v. 3).

Let us become concerned enough with the great doctrines of the Word of God so that we do not treat them just as statements of fact. Rather, let us take them as kernels of living truth which will strengthen us as we meditate upon what they reveal to us of the love and power of the God and Father of our Lord Jesus Christ. In this spirit we shall have no difficulty in translating the living essence of doctrinal truth into the practical realm of experiential living. In this way we shall be drawn closer to Him who loves us and loosed us from our sins through His own blood—"the Lamb of God, which taketh away the sin of the world" (John 1:29)—Jesus of Nazareth, "the Son of the Highest" (Luke 1:32).

6

THE GOSPEL OF RESURRECTION

What was the central truth of the early apostles' preaching? What was the stimulus to the miraculous growth of the early church? What was the energizing force which spread the gospel across the face of the earth? The answer to all these questions is the Resurrection of Jesus Christ. "He is risen!" was the victorious cry of the early Christians, and they spread it to the ends of the earth.

Unless we accept what the Scriptures teach about the Resurrection, the entire Christian message virtually disintegrates. The whole preaching thrust of the apostolic age was based upon the fact that one quiet morning in an obscure garden man had vanquished his most feared enemy, the vaunted dark angel of death. Satan had defeated the first Adam in a garden ages before, and with his victory there commenced the reign of sin and death over mankind. But now in God's appointed time and plan Satan met the last Adam in still another garden, and death was "swallowed up in victory" (1 Corinthians 15:54).

Unfortunately, some persons have treated the Resurrection as just another doctrine, a creedal statement to be accepted rather than a logical and rational ground of personal hope. But to the apostles it was *the* basis of hope amid intense persecution and suffering.

The early Christians based their teaching of a future resurrection of the dead upon the validity of the Resurrection of the Messiah of Israel, "the firstfruits of them that slept" (1 Corinthians 15:20,23). As Christ rose, they argued, so will He call all men to physical life or "as in Adam all die, even so in Christ shall all be made alive" (1 Corinthians 15:22).

Certainly Christianity is a creed to be believed, but it is also a life to be lived. Apart from the risen Savior the creed becomes a hollow sham and the life a struggle to lift oneself by one's own bootstraps. Christianity is above all a Person, and this Person is the Son of God.

Unfortunately, some doubt or reject the Resurrection altogether. Since the Resurrection predicates the miraculous, it repels the rationalistic mind of man. When Paul preached it, he was mocked and scorned by the Greek philosophers of his day (Acts 17:32), and on another occasion madness was ascribed to him by a pagan ruler (Acts 26:24). We should not wonder, then, if men today do not believe in it! The Resurrection of Christ resists rather than encourages faith.

There are also many who claim to believe in Christ's Resurrection but who deny that it was a *bodily* resurrection. They claim instead that Christ's Resurrection was merely spiritual. However, they overlook the fact that the only type of resurrection which the Bible teaches is bodily in nature.

In both the Hebrew and the Greek language the term "resurrection," unless used figuratively, always refers to the body, *never* to the immaterial nature or soul of man. A simple perusal of Greek and Hebrew lexicons establishes this beyond reasonable doubt.

There can be no question but that our Lord anticipated rising in a physical form. On one occasion Christ stated, "Destroy this temple and in three days I will raise it up" (John 2:19). That our Lord referred to His body is clear from John's remark, "He spake of the temple of his body" (John 2:21).

Christ proved His physical conquest of death by appearing in bodily form, bearing the wounds of the Cross. Thomas, who could not fathom the Resurrection, demanded the "print of the nails" in which to put his fingers and the riven side into which to thrust his hand (John 20:25). When Christ offered His hands and His side to Thomas as tangible evidence, the doubter became the worshiper, "My Lord and my God!" (John 20:28).

At another time Jesus faced and addressed His trembling disciples, who were terrified, supposing "that they had seen a spirit" (Luke 24:37).

"And he said unto them . . . Behold my hands and my feet, that it is I myself: handle me, and see; for a spirit hath not flesh and bones, as ye see me have. And when he had thus spoken, he shewed them *his* hands and *his* feet" (Luke 24:38-40).

Here was no phantom or spirit but the glorified Messiah of prophecy, eternally risen from the grave. The Christ of the Resurrection ate "fish and a honeycomb," presented His body to be examined, and showed Himself alive with "many infallible proofs" (Acts 1:3).

His was no mere spiritual resurrection but a *bodily* resurrection and a triumph over the supposed destiny of the body, the grave.

In the light of these stupendous truths it is no wonder that the cowards who forsook their Master at Gethsemane became the conquerors of Pentecost and the apostolic age. Here were men who dared to die because they had experienced eternal life incarnate and knew that because Christ lived they would live also. Those who saw the risen Savior were never the same again, and it is the same with those today who see Him with the eye of faith. He has not changed. He is "the same yesterday, to-day, and for ever" (Hebrews 13:8).

Paul alone calls 500 witnesses (1 Corinthians 15:6) to swear to the validity of the Resurrection. Peter adopts it as his Pentecostal theme (Acts 3:15). John exults, "Our hands have handled, of the Word of Life" (1 John 1:1). Shoulder to shoulder with Stephen we can face the stones of an enraged mob, for Jesus is "standing on the right hand of God" (Acts 7:55). In His presence death loses its terror, for He is the Prince of Life.

Dr. Robert McCracken has pointed out that if Christ's Resurrection were not bodily, we could claim no more for Him than for any other good man — the survival of the soul. But because He alone triumphed eternally over the grave as a man, Christianity is indeed unique and the Resurrection is its most unique characteristic.

The Word of God constantly emphasizes the necessity of believing the historic doctrine of the Resurrection of Jesus Christ. God has made eternal salvation itself contingent upon accepting this fact. It is impossible to be flexible with this eternal truth which forms the basis of man's redemption.

In 1 Corinthians 15:17 Paul taught, "If Christ be not raised [raised bodily], your faith is vain, ye are *yet* in your sins."

In his Epistle to the Romans Paul taught, "That if thou shalt confess with thy mouth the Lord Jesus and shalt believe in thine heart that God hath raised him from the dead, thou shalt be saved" (Romans 10:9).

But today, sad to say, all too many who call themselves "Christians" reject this great truth.

Those who challenge the bodily Resurrection of Jesus Christ generally hold to the "spiritual resurrection" theory. Their theory is based on two arguments allegedly drawn from Scripture:

1. In John 20 and Luke 24 Mary Magdalene and Christ's disciples failed to recognize the risen Savior, and it is alleged therefore that Jesus was a "spirit" and did not have any identifiable form.

The key to understanding these passages is found in a most revealing phrase—in Luke 24:16 "their eyes were holden" (literally "veiled" or "kept from recognizing Him"). Christ prevented His followers from learning His identity by an act of His divine will until He had accomplished the purpose of stimulating faith in His conquest and mission.

In the instance of Mary Magdalene, the mention of her name brought recognition. Today, under hypnosis, a subject who has been given a post-hypnotic suggestion can be prevented from recognizing a close relative. If man can do this by hypnosis, surely the sovereign act of God's Son presents no barrier to intelligent faith. Christ merely willed that His disciples and Mary should not recognize Him even though they beheld Him. They were incapable of understanding or perceiving that it was He until His purpose had been accomplished. This certainly does not teach a "spirit resurrection" in the least, and the Greek bears this out incontrovertibly.

2. A second argument is based on four verses, three of which are in 1 Corinthians 15. These verses (44, 45, 50), speak of the resurrection of a "spiritual body" and are used to support the theory of the spirit-resurrection.

Although Paul used the word "spiritual," he attached the word "body" to it, indicating that it was not merely a spirit that was being spoken of. Christ did have a "spiritual body" or a glorified form which had changed, even as we will be changed at His coming, but Christ was not merely a spirit. Our Lord had a body, a physical form possessed of certain spiritual characteristics or attributes which enabled Him to appear or disappear at will and to enter locked rooms.

These facts explain 1 Corinthians 15:50, for Christ possessed no blood, only "flesh and bones," and His flesh itself had undergone a miraculous change (incorruptibility) so that He and eventually His church might inherit the kingdom of God.

First Corinthians 15:45, "The first man Adam was made a living soul; the last Adam *was made* a quickening spirit," refers to Christ as a quickening spirit. Our Lord Himself enunciated this teaching when speaking of His authority as a life-giving spirit (John 5:21). In the Gospel of John He declares His power to quicken whom He wills. Christ also connected this to the resurrection of all flesh (John 5:25-29), underscoring one of His functions as the incarnate Logos (John 1:1,14).

The fourth verse used in this argument is 1 Peter 3:18 — ". . . being put to death in the flesh, but quickened by the Spirit."

Does this teach a spiritual rather than a bodily resurrection? By no means! Romans 8:11 tells us that it was in and through the Holy Spirit that the Lord Jesus Christ was raised from the dead: "But if the Spirit of him that raised up Jesus from the dead dwell in you . . .he also shall quicken your mortal bodies." It is evident that "likewise" means "in like manner"; just as the Spirit made Christ's body alive at His Resurrection, so will He make us alive in Christ.

Even as the Trinity was present in the Incarnation and baptism of the Savior, so it was present in His Resurrection. Christ stated, "I have power to lay it [my life] down, and I have power to take it again" (John 10:18). Peter confirmed that God the Father "raised up his Son Jesus" from among the dead (Acts 3:26). And in Romans 8:11 as well as in 1 Peter 3:18, the Holy Spirit is the medium of our Lord's conquest of the grave.

So the testimony of Scripture clearly proclaims the doctrine of the bodily Resurrection of Jesus Christ (Luke 24:37, 39).

But our Lord's Resurrection is far more than just a doctrinal proposition. It is the basic pillar upon which rests the hope of all Christians. Paul wrote, "And if Christ be not raised, your faith is vain; ye are yet in your sins" (1 Corinthians 15:17).

Christ was born, lived, suffered, died, and was resurrected as a man and as man's representative. Adam's sin had barred man from his fellowship with a holy God, but the last Adam's substitutionary sacrifice for sin made possible full reconciliation to God and the restoration of that lost fellowship (Hebrews 2:17).

The writer of Hebrews tells us that Christ through His Incarnation and by His death purposed to "render powerless" the one who possessed the power of death, that is, the Devil (Hebrews 2:14). In human form God the Son was manifested; in human form God the Son suffered and died; in human form God the Son was destined to triumph as a glorified, immortal man whose image the redeemed of the Lord will one day bear (1 John 3:2).

Jesus Christ, the eternal Logos and incarnate Son, accepted forever the limitation of perfect human nature for the sake of our redemption, and He retains for all eternity the identifying marks of His incarnate extension in time. Such love as this entitles Him to our everlasting gratitude and praise. He is indeed justly crowned "Lord of Life who triumphed over the grave, Creator of the rolling spheres, the ineffably sublime Potentate of time." As the hymn reminds us, "He lives that death may die."

Dr. B. F. Westcott once wrote:

> If the Resurrection be not true, the basis of Christian morality, no less than the basis of Christian theology, is gone. The issue cannot be stated too broadly. . . . *To preach the fact* of Resurrection was the first function of the Evangelists; *to embody the doctrine* of the Resurrection is the great office of the Church; *to learn the meaning* of the Resurrection is the task not of one age only, but of all.[1]

These words claim afresh the message of the early church as it preached the gospel of an immortal Redeemer in human form, our "great high priest, that is passed into the heavens, Jesus the Son of God" (Hebrews 4:14).

The writer of Hebrews has imparted to us that triumphant note of certainty which so characterized the early church when he stated, "Let us hold fast to *our* profession" (Hebrews 14:14). Christianity has survived because it has believed and confessed its faith in a resurrected Savior who alone among the children of men could say, "I am the resurrection, and the life" (John 11:25). Here is the key to a dynamic and vital faith—"He is risen." There is joy to the world, for the Lord has come indeed.

CHAPTER NOTE

1. B.F. Westcott, *The Gospel of the Resurrection* (New York: Macmillan, 1902), pp. 6-7.

7

SOVEREIGN GRACE AND HUMAN WORKS

The modern world of today, caught up in the tension and struggle of economics and political ideologies, moves more and more each year in the direction of automation. Almost every area of our lives has begun to feel this drive.

We constantly hear of automation in labor, as mechanical devices replace the worker; in electronics, where computers do the work of a hundred men in minutes; and in the business world, where technological progress has literally revolutionized countless enterprises from the ground up.

With such advances in our economic structure, everyday living in a country such as America has also seen a rapid revolution taking place.

Supermarkets have largely replaced the corner grocer, chains of dry-cleaners the local tailor shop, and self-shopping centers the formerly invincible department store. But in the midst of all this change, one factor remains constant and necessary to all, and that is the very necessary factor of credit.

Whether it be the MasterCard, VISA, Diners Club, American Express, Carte Blanche, and layaway plans right down to the old-fashioned charge account at the local store, everything moves on credit. This credit, for all its complicated financial computations and efficiency bureaus, is still based essentially on faith —faith that the purchaser will honor his word and meet his obligation if at all possible.

In a real sense this is all quite analogous to the Biblical doctrine of grace, which has been accurately defined as "the unmerited favor of God."

The New Testament faithfully expresses the divine will when it declares that "it is by grace you have been saved, through faith and that not by yourselves, for it is the gift of God, not through works, lest anyone should boast" (Ephesians 2:8,9, literal translation).

The sovereign grace of God (and it is sovereign or irresistible because mankind is its recipient wholly apart from merit) is the agency by which men are finally redeemed. Grace is fully manifested in the form of faith or, more properly, "repentance toward God and faith toward our Lord Jesus Christ" (Acts 20:21).

The New Testament reminds us that God justifies men *only through His grace* expressed in mercy (Titus 3:5), sacrifice (Romans 5:9), faith (Romans 5:1), and finally works (James 2:24).

According to Scripture it is solely by grace that God shows mercy to a race deserving eternal judgment for the rejection of His Son. This benevolent mercy in turn produces faith in men who will believe in the atoning sacrifice of His Son for their sins, and as a result it produces good works indicative of true repentance or proves repentance by deeds (Acts 26:20; Ephesians 2:10).

Lest there be any confusion at this point, let us clearly grasp the fact that so-called "good works" can *never* save or justify the soul before God. In his Epistle to Titus, Paul declares that salvation is *not* the result of any "works of righteousness which we have done" (3:5), and in Galatians he reinforces this by stating that "no man is justified by the law in the sight of God, . . . for, The just shall live by faith" (Galatians 3:11).

This extremely dogmatic teaching runs throughout the entire New Testament, particularly in what is termed "Pauline theology," a fact evidenced by his preoccupation with it in Romans, Galatians, Ephesians, and, oddly enough, with its practical application in the Epistle to Philemon.

But to return to the core of the matter, "good works" justify us before *men* in that they give tangible proof of our prior justification before God, which is solely on the basis of our faith in the Lord Jesus Christ.

The New English Bible beautifully captures the meaning of the Greek original when it states, "We know that no man is ever justified by doing what the law demands, but only through faith in Jesus Christ, in order that we might be justified through *this* faith" (Galatians 2:16).

The Apostle carries this out to its logical conclusion when in the same chapter he teaches that the Christian's "present bodily life is lived by faith in the Son of God" (Galatians 2:20 NEB), a faith which has as its natural outgrowth "a pattern of good works" (Titus 2:7). This is that abiding fruit produced by grace and faith which our Savior so pointedly emphasized (John 15:4,5).

We must understand, then, that faith and works can never in themselves (or together, for that matter) save anyone. It is sovereign grace *alone* that forms the basis for eternal salvation.

Good works "complete" the testimony of faith by witnessing to the fact of that faith's existence; they serve to justify us before *men,* who cannot *see* the grace or the faith that has already justified us before God. Our Lord taught that if we love Him and are in truth His disciples, we will obey Him. Therefore it is necessary for us not only to proclaim the fact of our salvation and justification, but to live lives that will reveal by their very content and devotion the truth of our profession. Unregenerate men cannot perceive the reality of our faith apart from our works performed for Christ. Such works have no merit in themselves, the Scripture reminds us (Ephesians 2:9), but they do indeed "justify" our faith and testify to its existence before a skeptical and hostile world.

This is the whole sense of the Apostle James' scathing pronouncement that "as the body without the spirit is dead, so faith without works is dead also" (James 2:26).

James *never* taught that works justify the soul before God, as some who ignore the context of his remarks and the complete meaning of justification *(before* God and *before* man) imply, for he was well acquainted with Paul's teaching on the subject and concurred in it. James certainly did *not* contradict Paul. It was James and Peter, in fact, who interviewed Paul after his conversion (Galatians 1:18,19) and later on, as Paul put it, "perceived the grace that was given unto me . . . and God gave to me . . . the right hand of fellowship; that we *should go* unto the heathen, and they unto the circumcision" (Galatians 2:9,10).

Peter held Paul's theology in such high esteem that, writing as "a pillar of the church" (Galatians 2:9), he described Paul as "our beloved brother" who "wrote to you with his inspired wisdom, as he does in all his other letters . . ." (2 Peter 3:15,16 NEB). It is quite evident, therefore, that there was unanimity on the part of the apostles where the relationship of grace and faith to works was concerned, and for all of them it was grace throughout. Faith, it is true, has its roots in grace, as does mercy, and good works are most certainly the result, but grace and grace alone redeems. And so in the most powerful sense of that term's meaning, grace is truly sovereign.

Those who advocate the concept that works produce merit, which in cooperation with grace and faith result in final salvation for the sinner (as in Roman Catholicism), will find no support in Pauline theology for such speculations. While it is true that Christians will stand in judgment for the works performed after acceptance of Christ as Savior ("the deeds done in the body"), it is *not* true that this judgment will affect their eternal destiny.

Scripture is careful to point out that "there is therefore now no judgment unto death for those who are in Christ Jesus"

(Romans 8:1, literal translation), and Christ Himself taught that whoever "hears my word and believes Him who sent me has eternal life and shall never come into judgment unto death but has passed out of death into life" (John 5:24, literal translation).

Here then is real security and salvation that is truly eternal because it rests upon the word of One who is Himself eternal "after the power of indissoluble life" (Hebrews 7:16, literal translation).

Lest there be a misunderstanding here, we hasten to point out that one cannot accept Christ with all that this act entails and then say, "Now that I am forever saved, I can sin with impunity and never be lost." Christ taught that if we love Him our love will manifest itself in obedience and conformity to the will of God. The Savior said, "If ye love me, keep my commandments" (John 14:15), and all His commandments were condensed under the heading, "Thou shalt love the Lord thy God with all thy heart, and with all thy soul, and with all thy mind. . . . Thou shalt love thy neighbour as thyself." On this "hang all the law and the prophets" (Matthew 22:37-40).

Paul writes that "love is the fulfilling of the law" (not its destruction) and that the law of God is established and its righteousness fulfilled in the lives of those who have been justified by faith in Jesus Christ (Romans 13:10). All law, the Apostle teaches, "is fulfilled in love" (Romans 13:10 NEB), and all commandments may be "summed up in one rule, you shall love your neighbor as yourself" (Romans 13:9 NEB). This led the great theologian Augustine to state in answer to the question, "How shall we obey God's law?" — "Love God and do as you please." What he meant was clear to all but his enemies, for Augustine had grasped one of the greatest of all truths in Scripture, namely, that, if we truly love God, we will do those things that please Him. True love, as Christ and the apostles taught it, was just that simple. If we love Him and our neighbor as ourselves, we will both please God and deal honorably with all men apart from any restrainer, for "the law is not made for a righteous man, but for the lawless" (1 Timothy 1:9) and in Christ we are "dead indeed unto sin" (Romans 6:11) and alive to its righteousness, which is fulfilled in us "who walk not after the flesh, but after the Spirit" (Romans 8:4).

Thus it is that the "law of the Spirit of life in Christ Jesus hath made me free from the law of sin and death" (Romans 8:2) and Christ has fulfilled all law in our behalf by dying in our stead.

The Lord Jesus said that the love of Christians one for another would be the seal of our discipleship to the unbelieving world, and He went so far as to explicitly describe it as "a new commandment" (John 13:34,35).

The Bible teaches incontrovertibly that "Christ is the end of the law as a way of righteousness for everyone who has faith" (Romans 10:4a NEB), and that whereas the law once acted as a tutor to lead us to Christ, now that He has appeared the law has been fulfilled and the tutor is no longer over us (Galatians 3:25). Far from destroying the law, then, Christ fulfilled it perfectly to "the jot and tittle,"and then it ceased its function as tutor. In effect, the shadow disappeared because the substance which projected it had appeared as God incarnate (Colossians 2:17; John 1:1,14). Those who make statements about license for scandalous conduct on the part of so-called Christians have never really understood what it means to be redeemed.

Those who have been redeemed know that "the love of Christ [not the fear of the law] constraineth us" (2 Corinthians 5:14) and fulfills the righteousness of the law of God in our lives, so that we obey out of love for Him who "first loved us" (1 John 4:19) and sent His Son to be our Savior.

Christians are, of course, not exempt from sinning, and that is precisely the reason God provided for our sins through confession of those sins to Him. When this is done in earnest repentance and faith, the Scripture declares "the blood of Jesus Christ, His Son, *keeps on cleansing* us from *all* sin" (1 John 1:7,9, literal translation).

No true Christian can claim redemption in Christ through the new birth from above (1 Peter 1:23) but still habitually practice or be dominated by sin while claiming to have been saved never to be lost again. One has never been saved if he speaks and acts like this, for, as John reminds us, "he that is born from God does not practice sin habitually, for his seed remains in him" (1 John 3:9, literal translation). Let it never be forgotten that profession of a saving experience with Christ does *not* necessarily mean that one has been redeemed. John cautions us about pseudo-Christians, of whom he says, "They went out from our company but never really belonged to us, for if they had, they would have stayed with us, but they went out that it might be clear that not all in our company truly belong to it" (1 John 2:19 NEB).

The apostle of love, as John has sometimes been called, could more than live up to the nickname "son of thunder" which our Lord gave him!

In this same Epistle, speaking of false Christians who professed to know Christ and acted otherwise, John thundered: "And hereby we do know that we know him, if we keep his commandments. He that saith I know him, and keepeth not his commandments, is a liar, and the truth is not in him. But whoso keepeth his word, in him verily is the love of God perfected: hereby know we that we are in him. He that saith he abideth in him ought himself also so to walk even as he walked. . . . Let us not love in word, neither in tongue; but in deed and in truth. . . . He that loveth not knoweth not God; for God is love" (1 John 2:3-6; 3:18; 4:8).

That there would be no possibility of misinterpreting his repeated usage of "keeping Christ's commandments," John defines carefully for us what he means, "And this commandment have we from him, That he who loveth God love his brother also" (1 John 4:21).

John's concept of "keeping commandments" is the same as Paul's; he introduces no new thought, as he himself stated in 1 John 2:7. Once again, grace working through love fulfills the requirements of the Christian life, for if we are truly loving God and our neighbor as ourselves, we will always be found in harmony with all of God's laws.

The Son of God sobers us with the statement that we are not to call Him Lord and "do *not* the things which I say" (Luke 6:46), for true love is witnessed *to* and demonstrated *by* obedience, "for obedience is better than sacrifice, and to listen to the Lord better than the sacrifice of rams" (1 Samuel 15:22, literal translation).

In concluding this chapter, we must return once again to the illustration of credit and charge accounts for the final proof of our central thesis, the absolute sovereignty of grace as one of the unshakable foundations of essential Christianity. There can be no mixture of grace and works in the divine economy of redemption. As we have seen, this is "another gospel," and Paul did not shrink from pronouncing a double curse in the strongest possible terms upon anyone who promulgated this well-known error of the Galatians (Galatians 1:8,9).

But how does this gospel of grace operate in practical experience? It may sound good, many say, but does it work? The Apostle Paul provides us with the answer to these questions.

In the third and fourth chapter of Romans, Paul cites David and Abraham as the prime examples of how God saves and justifies men by grace and also how God deals with the sins of those whom He justifies.

But now, quite independently of law, God's justice has been brought to light. The Law and the prophets both bear witness to it: It is God's way of righting wrong, effective through faith in Christ for all who have such faith — all, without distinction. For all alike have sinned, and are deprived of the divine splendour, and all are justified by God's free grace alone, through his act of liberation in the person of Christ Jesus. For God designed him to be the means of expiating sin by his sacrificial death, effective through faith. God meant by this to demonstrate his justice, because in his forbearance he had overlooked the sins of the past — to demonstrate his justice now in the present, showing that he is himself just and justifies any man who puts his faith in Jesus.

What room then is left for human pride? It is excluded. And on what principle? The keeping of the law would not exclude it, but faith does.

For our argument is that a man is justified by faith quite apart from success in keeping the law. . . .

Does this mean that we are using faith to undermine law? By no means: we are placing law itself on a firmer footing. . . .

What then, are we to say about Abraham, our ancestor in the natural line? If Abraham was justified by anything he had done, then he has a ground for pride. But he has no such ground before God; for what does Scripture say? "Abraham put his faith in God, and that faith was counted to him as righteousness." Now if a man does a piece of work, his wages are not "counted" as a favour; they are paid as debt. But if without any work to his credit he simply puts his faith in him who acquits the guilty, then his faith is indeed "counted as righteousness." In the same sense David speaks of the happiness of the man whom God "counts" as just, apart from any specific acts of justice: "Happy are they," he says, "whose lawless deeds are forgiven, whose sins are buried away; happy is the man whose sins the Lord does not count against him." Is this happiness confined to the circumcised, or is it for the uncircumcised also? Consider: we say, "Abraham's faith was counted as righteousness"; . . . but where there is no law there can be no breach of law. The promise was made on the ground of faith, in order that it might be a matter of sheer grace, and that it might be valid for all Abraham's posterity, not only for those who hold by the law, but for those also who have the faith of Abraham. For he is the father of us all, as Scripture says: . . . Without any weakening of faith he contemplated his own body, as good as dead (for he was about a hundred years old), and the deadness of Sarah's womb, and never doubted God's promise in unbelief, but, strong in faith, gave honour to God, in the firm conviction of his power to do what he had promised. And that is why Abraham's faith was "counted to him as righteousness."

Those words were written, not for Abraham's sake alone, but for our sake too: it is to be "counted" in the same way to us who have faith in the God who raised Jesus our Lord from the dead; for he was given up to death for our misdeeds, and raised to life to justify us (Romans 3:21-28, 31; 4:1-9,15-17,19-25 NEB).

Note carefully that if we could earn our salvation in any way then grace would be annulled, for then it is no longer the *gift* of God but a *debt* which God owes to us (v. 4). Paul goes on to point out that a man's faith in Christ is counted by God as the supreme work of righteousness (v. 5) and that the Lord, as in the case of David, counts a man just "apart from any specific act of justice. . . . Happy is the man whose sins the Lord does not count against him" (vv. 6, 8).

With unflinching courage the inspired Apostle expounds the breathtaking doctrine that "a man is justified by faith quite apart from success in keeping the law" (Romans 3:28, literal translation). By such an act of sovereign grace God's justice is brought to light, the law and the prophets bearing witness to it, "showing that He himself is both just and justifies anyone who puts his faith in Jesus" (Romans 3:26, literal translation).

The purpose of all this, Paul tells us, is that God promised Abraham redemption *because* of his faith, so that all those who accept God's promise in Christ might be "as a matter of sheer grace" (Romans 4:16, literal translation) children of Abraham by faith, having their faith counted as righteousness even as was Abraham's (Romans 4:22).

Here is the triumph of sovereign grace. God has promised to consider as righteous those who are in themselves unrighteous, simply because they put their faith in His Son, who died for the ungodly, "the just for the unjust, that he might bring us to God" (1 Peter 3:18).

How true it is that God made Him to become sin for us, He "who knew no sin; that we might be made the righteousness of God in him" (2 Corinthians 5:21). It is Christ's perfection then that is imputed to our record. It is Christ's perfection that clothes our imperfection, and it is Christ's blood that cleanses us from all sin and makes us acceptable to God by faith. Such is the inexhaustible credit of grace the redeemed have in heaven. This is the divine charge account (measureless grace) imputed and imparted by faith in Jesus Christ alone.

In his classic Epistle to Philemon, Paul pleads for Onesimus, the runaway slave and one of his converts. It is the Apostle's wish that Philemon, his master, may receive him back as a Christian brother and waive the death penalty or other punishment due under Roman law to those who fled slavery.

Toward the end of the letter Paul injects a sentence which, more than any other in the New Testament, in my opinion, exemplifies the practical outworking of sovereign grace.

> If, then, you count me partner in the faith, welcome him as you would welcome me. And if he has done you any wrong or is in your debt, put

that down to my account. Here is my signature, PAUL; I undertake to repay — not to mention that you owe your very self to me as well. Now, brother, as a Christian, be generous with me, and relieve my anxiety; we are both in Christ!

I write to you confident that you will meet my wishes; I know that you will in fact do better than I ask. And one thing more: have a room ready for me, for I hope that, in answer to your prayers, God will grant me to you (Philemon 17-22 NEB).

It is of great significance that Paul reminds Philemon, evidently a Roman nobleman of some importance, that he owes his own salvation to Paul's ministry and that if Onesimus owes him anything, then it is to be charged or put to Paul's account and reckoned as paid in full. What a beautiful picture that is of God's gracious love to us in Christ! He has put to the account of His own Son, our passover lamb, all our sins, and Christ by paying the supreme penalty once-for-all has purchased by the ransom of His own blood redemption by grace alone and justification before God for "those who put their faith in Jesus" (Romans 3:26 NEB).

We may know, then, through these great and precious truths that in Christ we, like Abraham and David of old, can stand whole and complete in the Father's presence. We can cross over the bridge of doubt that spans the chasm of fear, and we can indeed be at peace with God through our Lord Jesus Christ (Romans 5:1).

We may know with absolute certainty that the promises made to Abraham and David are ours also by faith, and that Jesus was delivered to death for our misdeeds and raised to life to justify us (Romans 4:23-25).

Knowing all these things, we can fully appreciate *all* the bills which human sin has amassed, saying with Paul of old, "Who shall charge anything to God's elect? It is Christ who justifies. ..." It is no less than God the Son who says, "Put that on my account — I have signed it with my own hand, JESUS" (Romans 8:33,34; Philemon 19, free rendering).

Here is the triumph of grace and the fruit of faith; here is victory and freedom; here alone is peace with God.

8

THE CHRISTIAN AND SPIRITUAL GIFTS

In the Christian world today "spiritual gifts" have become *the* topic of conversation. Agreeing with the Apostle Paul that "there must be also heresies among you, that they which are approved may be made manifest among you" (1 Corinthians 11:9), it is important that the issue and its Biblical ramifications be understood and appreciated.

The New Testament speaks of certain "gifts" bestowed by God the Holy Spirit upon the church of Jesus Christ. In Romans 12:6, for instance, it is mentioned that each member of the church or body of Christ possesses different gifts "according to the grace that is given to us." In Ephesians 4:8, Paul further writes that God "gave gifts unto men," and in 1 Corinthians 12:1 he adds, "Now concerning spiritual *gifts,* brethren, I would not have you ignorant."

Throughout church history Christians in general have recognized these gifts in one manner or another, and beyond reasonable doubt they have believed that they are a definite part of the spiritual inheritance of all true Christians. Certainly these gifts existed in the early church, and there is no logical, historical, or exegetical reason for supposing that they were *not* intended to exist in either greater or lesser measure so long as that church would endure on the earth.

The Apostle Paul stressed quite heavily the importance of spiritual gifts, particularly those known as charismatic gifts or "the gifts of grace." "For to one is given by the Spirit the word of wisdom; to another the word of knowledge by the same Spirit; to another faith by the same Spirit; and to another the gifts of healing by the same Spirit; to another the working of miracles; to another prophecy; to another discerning of spirits; to another *divers* kinds of tongues; to another the interpretation of tongues: But all these worketh that one and the selfsame Spirit, dividing to every man severally as he will" (1 Corinthians 12:8-11).

Paul not only announces that there are spiritual gifts manifested by the Holy Spirit, but he also teaches that there are varieties of gifts (v. 4), varieties of service (v. 5), and varieties of operation concerning these gifts (v. 6), and that the manifestation of the Spirit is given to profit the entire church or body (v. 7).

Paul goes on to declare that all of these manifestations are from the same Spirit and are manifested through the one body (the church).

In the last one hundred years some theologians have found it fashionable to resurrect old and discredited arguments to the effect that the gifts of the Spirit ceased with the apostolic church. But from the standpoint of sound exegesis, history, and comparative textual analysis *in context,* such a position is highly speculative and is totally unwarranted by the Biblical, historical, and contemporary evidence at hand.

One of the chief objections to the gifts of the Spirit in the Christian church today, for example, is based upon 1 Corinthians 13:8-10 (literal translation):

"Love never faileth: but whether there be prophecies, they shall fail; whether there be tongues, they shall cease; whether there be knowledge, it shall vanish away."

However, if we take this verse to mean that the gift of tongues and the gift of prophecy have ceased, it must also follow logically from the context that the gift of knowledge has also vanished away! If this is so, we must explain in some other way the manifestation of this obvious gift as well as other gifts in the lives and ministries of the great giants of the Christian church throughout the ages. Those who attempt this are on vulnerable ground indeed.

Some who would do away with spiritual gifts for our age contend further that 1 Corinthians 13:10 vindicates their position:

"But when that which is *perfect* is come, then that which is in part shall be done away." These brethren insist that this verse refers *not* to the termination of the gifts at the Second Advent (which is the classical interpretation) but instead to either the *completion* of the New Testament canon or the apostolic era!* Consequently, they conclude that it was unnecessary for the gifts of the Spirit to continue. This, we maintain, is a very weak assumption, unsupported by the context and language of the chapter. While it is true that love is the fulfillment — yes, the consummation — of all spiritual gifts, it is *not* stated nor is it implied that love is intended to supersede the gifts of the Holy Spirit, but rather that the gifts are to be *exercised in love* and in accordance with God's commands. This is a far cry from assigning the arbitrary interpretation to the New Testament canon, a thought entirely foreign to the Greek in the context, but one which the late Benjamin Warfield popularized and succeeded in virtually canonizing itself.

The late Dr. A. J. Gordon once made some pertinent observations on this very subject.

> The promise of miracles is to the faithful as a body. The church has come into existence so soon as any had believed and had been baptized; and thus this guarantee of miraculous signs seems to be to the church in its

---

*Much is made of the neuter gender in this verse, but since the event of the Second Coming is in view here (rather than explicitly the Person of Jesus Christ), this gender harmonizes well with the classical view.

corporate capacity. "Are all workers of miracles? Have all the gifts of healing? Do all speak with tongues?" asks the Apostle (1 Corinthians 12:29,30). Nay, but some employ these offices so that the gifts are to be found in the church as a whole.

Expanding on this subject, Dr. Gordon further declares: "The bounds set to the exercise of these gifts is when 'that which is perfect is come,' which scholarship has generally held to mean when the Lord Himself shall return to earth. The gifts of tongues and of prophecy therefore do not seem to be confined within the first age of the church."

There is a wealth of information on this subject from renowned scholarly and exegetical commentaries, the overwhelming majority of which espouse the position of Dr. Gordon on excellent grammatical grounds. It is sufficient to note that none of them risk the interpretations given to 1 Corinthians 13:10 that some Biblical expositors have hazarded over the last one hundred years.

Many noted authorities, when commenting upon 1 Corinthians 13:8-10, link it with a number of Biblical passages which, all agree, deal with the Second Advent of Christ and the consummation of the age. The margins of most Bibles connect 1 Corinthians 13:10 and 1 John 3:2 together without hesitation, so obvious is it that the termination of the gifts is to take place at the Second Advent. We see, then, that the context of 1 Corinthians 13 is clarified particularly by verse 12. Far from referring to verse 8 as the cessation of the New Testament era or the apostolic authority, or to the completion of the canon of Scripture, verse 12 teaches that the gifts will cease their full manifestation when we see "face to face" and when "we know even as also we are known." This statement is grammatically inseparable from the concept of the Second Advent of our Lord. If it is to be considered separately, then we must be prepared to believe that Paul was in error, because in verse 12, following the dispensational interpretation, Paul said he would "know" when the canon closed or the apostolic age closed — but he died at least

25 years *before* the close of the Canon and 35 years before the close of the apostolic age (90 A.D.)! This interpretation does not fit the context, and it is the Second Advent ("face to face" with Christ) that Paul here intends to convey. (See Calvin's commentary on this point.)

Those who would restrict spiritual gifts to apostolic times (gifts originating with God the Holy Spirit) should seek stronger ground than such standard or stock references previously mentioned, though such strong ground is conspicuously absent from the New Testament Epistles. In fact, let it be understood that for Paul "the gifts and calling of God are irrevocable" (Romans 11:29, literal translation), that is, not bound to any one age any more than the covenant made with Abraham was bound by that age. To maintain that spiritual gifts have ceased in the Christian church, therefore, is to go contrary to sound Scriptural evidence. First Corinthians 12 clearly teaches us that the Holy Spirit does manifest Himself to Christians in specific orders of gifts and as He pleases. Let us not forget that it was the Lord Jesus Himself who said the Spirit blows where He wills (John 3:8).

Of course, there have been and still are abuses of spiritual gifts by some believers, even as there is neglect of these gifts by other believers. However, neither neglect nor abuse negates the Spirit's moving, for by virtue of His omnipotence He can do anything today which He has done in the past. That these gifts may be neglected is clear from 1 Timothy 4:14, "Neglect not the gift that is in thee," and 2 Timothy 1:6, "Stir up the gift of God." But neglect is *not* denial, and it is with denial that we are primarily concerned.

FRUIT AND GIFTS

Lest we be carried away into a confusion of terminology, we must understand the difference between "the fruit of the Spirit" and "the gifts of the Spirit." In Galatians 5, Paul carefully differentiates between the fruit of the Spirit and the gifts of the Spirit for a very important reason, "But the fruit of the Spirit is love, joy, peace, longsuffering, gentleness, goodness, faith, meekness, temperance" (vv. 22, 23); but he also comments that "the fruit of the Spirit is in all goodness and righteousness and truth" (Ephesians 5:9,10).

The "fruit of the Spirit" is to be evidenced in the life of *every* believer as proof of the transforming power of the new birth. On the other hand, the gifts of the Spirit are bestowed as the Spirit wills, and not *all* believers receive the same gifts. This distinction is carefully maintained throughout the New Testament references relevant to the subject.

Since 1 Corinthians 12, in conjunction with Romans 11:29, teaches the perpetuity of God's gifts, some Christian groups maintain that they have the right to claim these gifts on what unfortunately amounts to an exclusive basis. Seventh-day Adventists, for instance, maintain that the "gift of prophecy" has been manifested in the life and teaching of Ellen G. White, the most influential single force in their history. The Adventists cite Revelation 19:10 in support of this position.

> And I fell at his feet to worship him. And he said unto me, See thou do it not: I am thy fellowservant, and of thy brethren that have the testimony of Jesus: worship God: for the testimony of Jesus is *the spirit of prophecy*" (emphasis added).

Comparing this verse with 1 Corinthians 12, the Adventists contend that Mrs. White possessed that very "spirit of prophecy," the true testimony of Jesus, and that this fact entitles them to the singular honor of being the "remnant church" of Revelation 12:17.

While we cannot rightfully challenge the *possibility* of the manifestation of the "gift of prophecy," we must clearly understand what the word "prophecy" means in the Greek. Actually its primary meaning is that of foretelling a given event as a result of knowledge imparted from God. Consider, for example, the Old Testament prophecies concerning the birth, death, and resurrection of our Lord. However, the word also means proclaiming or reiterating something God has said in the past, with a contemporary application as the Spirit leads. This thought we find running through the entire Bible in line with the clear revelation of God. Although the Adventists have the right to accept the "gift of prophecy," we most strenuously object to any Adventists' attempts to pressure the entire Christian church with the counsel contained in the writings of Mrs. White. Let us not forget that many students of Adventism and of the writings of the alleged "spirit of prophecy" doubt the reliability of many of Mrs. White's counsels. Contradictions in definite areas, as well as exegetical conflict, also exist within certain of these allegedly inspired utterances. We are therefore correct in questioning their supposedly divine origin.* The question, in the case of Seventh-Day Adventism, is not "Does the gift of prophecy exist?" but "Did it exist in the life and ministry of Ellen G. White?" Does it exist in the measure claimed by the Seventh-Day Adventists and by certain other groups? On the whole we consider the evidence both sketchy and overly mystical in nature as well as Biblically undemonstrable — hence our rejection of these claims.

HEALING AND TONGUES MOVEMENTS

In the area of spiritual gifts there are many Pentecostal and Holiness groups which emphasize the gift of healing and "baptism in the Holy Spirit," initially evidenced by speaking in "unknown tongues."

Admittedly divine healing, a gift from God, does exist in our age as one of the gifts of the Spirit, as previously mentioned. But we must be quick to compare the methods, promises, and doctrines of many so-called healers against the Biblical position. Healing is a gift from God and is always in accordance with His will (John 14:13,14; 1 John 5:14). It is never to be hawked as an attendance-raising or fund-raising expedient — a lamentable practice of many so-called healers. We must face the fact that

---

*See my book *The Kingdom of the Cults* (Minneapolis: Bethany Fellowship, 1977), Appendix A.

there are some believers whom God permits to be sick or deformed (Exodus 4:11), as well as those whom Satan and their own sins render ill (Isaiah 38:1; Job 2:7; John 5:14; John 9:3; 1 Corinthians 11:29,30). Sickness is a many-sided problem indeed. It cannot be met by the prevailing oversimplification of blaming all diseases on demons or on lack of faith on the part of the afflicted!

We can assuredly know that God heals when He wills and at His discretion. To be sure, faith plays a vital part, as our Lord said: "Thy faith hath saved thee...thy faith hath made thee whole, ..." But unless it is in accordance with His will, even the greatest faith is insufficient.

The great error of some of those who maintain the existence of the gifts of the Spirit within the present-day constituency of the body of Christ is that they tend to become exclusivistic and inordinately proud of their claim to special gifts. They lapse quite often into a judgmental type of Christianity bordering on acute Pharisaism, thus tending to reduce other Christians to a second-class citizenship. Going beyond this, they sometimes magnify one or another of the spiritual gifts out of all proportion to its Biblical importance. In so doing, they neglect Paul's pointed counsel:

> But all these [the gifts] worketh that one and selfsame Spirit, dividing to every man severally as he will. . . . For the body is not one member, but many. . . . But now hath God set the members every one of them in the body, as it hath pleased him . . . That there should be no schism in the body; but *that* the members should have the same care one for another. . . . Now ye are the body of Christ, and members in particular (1 Corinthians 12:11,14,18,25,27).

We see, then, that the Biblical position concerning the Christian's attitude toward spiritual gifts is that we cannot fairly or honestly challenge the existence of the gifts. But we should test both the gifts and those who profess to possess them by the Biblical standards of sound doctrine and fruitage. We ought never to forget the Apostle's injunction to seek for spiritual gifts as a means of power in the Christian life (1 Corinthians 14:1) so that God may minister to us through the Spirit to the fullest extent attainable. Certainly, great confusion can result from the abuse of the gifts of the Spirit, but to deny the functioning of the gifts of grace within the historic and contemporary Christian church, and to compound this error by attempting to "prove" it from Scripture, which speaks so clearly to the contrary, is indeed theological folly. It should never be forgotten that "God hath set some in the church . . . miracles, then gifts of healings, helps, governments, diversities of tongues. . . . Have all the gifts of healing? do all speak with tongues? do all interpret?" (1 Corinthians 12:28,30).

We ought to keep an open and balanced mind on this subject of the "charismata" or spiritual gifts, remembering, of course, the supreme imperative of love (1 Corinthians 13:13). It is this which compels us as our primary duty to love one another as Christ loved us and to preserve the unity of the body, "that there should be no schism in the body; but *that* the members should have the same care one for another" (1 Corinthians 12:25). This, we believe, is the key to understanding the relationship of the Christian to *all* of the gifts of the Spirit.

9

THE HOPE OF THE AGES

Students of the Bible throughout the ages have debated the great issues of theology with uncompromising vigor. But one major fact of New Testament revelation all agree that Christ believed in and taught — that He would return to earth a second time. It is perfectly true that some skeptical scholars have denied that this would take place (some have accused the evangelists and the apostles of myth-building or erecting a legend about the Person of Jesus), but none have denied that Christ Himself taught His personal second advent. A fact that fairly bristles from the pages of the Old and New Testaments is that God through His Messiah one day intends to judge the universe — angelic, demonic, and human — and to consummate the divine plan of the ages. Daniel the prophet, centuries before the birth of Jesus of Nazareth, predicted with more than human confidence that "I saw . . . and behold, *one* like the Son of man came with the clouds of heaven, and came to the Ancient of days, and they brought him near before him. And there was given him dominion, and glory, and a kingdom, that all people, nations, and languages, should serve him: his dominion *is* an everlasting dominion, which shall not pass away, and his kingdom *that* which shall not be destroyed'' (Daniel 7:13,14).

Isaiah, the prophet of incomparable stature in the Old Testament, declared of the Messiah: ''Of the increase of his government and peace *there shall be* no end, upon the throne of David, and upon his kingdom, to order it, and to establish it with judgment and with justice from henceforth even for ever. The zeal of the Lord of hosts will perform this'' (Isaiah 9:7).

In the twelfth chapter of the prophet Zechariah's revelations, these cryptic words continue to describe the moving specter of Messianic judgment: "In that day the Lord shall defend the inhabitants of Jerusalem; the one who is feeble among them in that day shall be like David, and the house of David like God, like the Angel of the Lord before them. In that day I shall seek to exterminate all the nations that come up against Jerusalem, and I shall pour out upon the house of David and upon the inhabitants of Jerusalem the spirit of grace and supplication, and they shall look upon Him Whom they have pierced, and they shall wail for Him as one wails for an only son, and they shall be in bitterness for Him like the bitterness for the firstborn" (Zechariah 12:8-10 *Berkeley Version*).

If we link this passage to Psalm 22 (where David speaks prophetically of the death of God's Son, the Messiah) and couple it with its fulfillment in John 19 and Revelation 1:7, there can be little doubt that the passage refers to Jesus of Nazareth, the One who was wounded, bruised, and put to death for the sins of Israel and the world (Isaiah 53; Daniel 9:26; 1 John 2:2).

Fantastic as it may seem, the prophetic theology of both the Old and New Testaments concerning the Messiah of Israel describes a Savior who first suffers for the sins of the world and then, because of His rejection by the world, returns to judge it. The hope of the ages, then, is the return of Jesus Christ — no longer the sinbearer and object of contempt and rejection by sinful and unappreciative men, but now the Sovereign Judge of the cosmos, whose glorious appearance will trigger the events known in Christian theology as "the day of the Lord."

It is quite natural that men who will not accept the love of God so openly displayed in the Person of our Savior, and who deny vehemently His Resurrection from the tomb, will continue to scoff at any suggestion of His return as their Judge. Consequently the Christian church has been taunted unceasingly by its critics, from the first century to the present day, concerning the return of the Master. But God has providentially both anticipated and answered their objections. The Apostle Peter put it this way:

I will therefore take care always to remind you of these matters, even though you are aware of them and are steady-minded in the truth now available. Still, I think it my duty, so long as I remain in this bodily tent, to keep you wide-awake by reminding you; for I know that shortly my body will be put off, as our Lord Jesus Christ made clear to me. Besides, I will make every effort to enable each one of you to keep these things in mind after I am gone; for when we acquainted you with the power and coming of our Lord Jesus Christ we were not accepting the authority of cleverly devised fables. On the contrary, we were eyewitnesses of His majesty, for as He was receiving honor and glory from God the Father, such a voice was borne to Him from the supreme glory, "This is My Son, My Beloved, in whom I am delighted." And we heard this voice borne to us from heaven when we were with Him on the sacred mountain. So we have the prophetic message reaffirmed, to which you do well to pay attention as you would to a light that shines in a dark place until the day dawns and the Daystar arises in your hearts, with this most clearly understood, that no prophetic Scripture can be explained by one's unaided mental powers. Because no prophecy ever resulted from human design; instead, holy men from God spoke as they were carried along by the Holy Spirit. . . . First of all you should understand that in the last days scoffers will come on the scene with their scoffing, behaving in line with their own lusts, and saying, "What about His promised coming? For ever since the forefathers fell asleep, everything has remained as it was from the beginning of creation." They willfully ignore the fact that from of old there were heavens, and an earth standing partly above and partly amidst water by the word of God, by means of which the then-existing world was destroyed, deluged as it was by water. At present, however, the heavens and the earth are by the same command stored up for burning and reserved for the day of judgment and the destruction of the godless people. Do not overlook this one fact, however, dear friends, that with the Lord one day is as a thousand years and a thousand years as one day. The Lord is not dawdling about His promise, as some think of dawdling; instead, He is exercising patience with you, desiring as He does that none should perish, but that all should come to repentance. But the day of the Lord will come like a thief. Then with a tremendous crash the heavens will pass away; the burning elements will be dissolved; the earth too and the works in it shall be burned up.

Since all these things are thus to be dissolved, how consecrated and reverent your behavior should be, as you are expecting and hastening on the coming day of God, on whose account the blazing heavens will be dissolved and the burning elements melted. But we are, in agreement with His promise, looking for new heavens and a new earth in which righteousness is at home (2 Peter 1:12-21; 3:3-13 *Berkeley Version*).

We can see clearly from the preceding testimony of Peter that we have been bequeathed no Grecian mythology or pseudo-mystical conjectures, but instead the sober truth, unbelievable though it may be to the always-skeptical mind of man, and we can see that there is both wisdom and great truth in the simplicity of its declaration.

We can learn from these inspired words, drawn from the life and experience of an old man and veteran of the faith, that God's concept of time is not our concept of time, and that if the universe is, as some scientists tell us, between four and eleven billion years old, then time to the Creator of the vast complexities of nature is purely relative and merely waits upon His pleasure to reach its consummation.

Our Lord Himself taught beyond question that His return to the earth to deliver His church, raise the dead, and establish the eternal reign of righteousness would be an event far in the future, though Christians were to live each day in the greatest expectation of its imminency. In one of His discourses recorded in Matthew's Gospel, Christ stated, "And this gospel of the kingdom shall be preached in all the world for a witness unto all nations; and then shall the end come" (Matthew 24:14).

It is quite obvious that His gospel has not yet been "preached in all the world for a witness unto all nations." And not until that day looms upon the horizon of history will His glorious advent take place.

Let us not be deceived by those who state, as does Dr. Rudolph Bultmann, that Jesus expected to return within the lifetime of the apostles and was unfortunately mistaken, or be swayed by those who so earnestly look for His return "any moment" that they lose sight of the responsibilities of the present day. We would do well to remember that the question which led to our Lord's answer was, "Tell us, when shall these things be? and what *shall be* the sign of thy coming, and of the end of the world?" (Matthew 24:3). The disciples genuinely wanted to know about the return of the Lord, and He answered them plainly and to the point. The twenty-fourth chapter of Matthew contains events which led up to the destruction of the temple at Jerusalem in 70 A.D. under the Emperor Titus, thus answering the disciples' first question concerning the destruction of the temple. But the chapter also contains prophecies concerning Christ's advent as King of Kings and Lord of Lords (Revelation 19:11-16) and is therefore relevant to the discussion of that which Paul describes to Titus as "the blessed hope" (Titus 2:13).

Let us not become so concerned with *when* our Lord is coming; rather, let us rejoice in the fact that He *is coming*, for we are to be always prepared so that we may not be ashamed at His appearance.

Another objection raised by critics of Christianity is that Christ said He would return before the generation in which He was living perished from the earth. They cite the accounts of both Mark and Luke (Mark 13:30; Luke 21:32).

Although this appears on the surface to be a formidable argument, a careful study of any good Greek lexicon of the New Testament will quickly show that the Greek word translated "generation" in the aforementioned passages (*genea*) can refer not only to those living at a specific time but also to those of a specific race — in this instance to the Jews. What our Lord was teaching was that the Jews as a nation would not pass from the earth until all of His prophecies had come to pass. The record of history validates our Lord's words. For the Jews have survived despite the Torquemadas, the Hitlers, the Stalins, and the Eichmanns, and they remain, as the great historian Arnold Toynbee has so graphically put it, "a fossil in the mainstream of history." When the whole record of the New Testament is carefully analyzed, one cannot escape the fact that our Lord Himself left the decision as to His return in the hands of His heavenly Father when He said, "But of that day and hour knoweth no *man,* no, not the angels of heaven, but my Father only" (Matthew 24:36).

Men have erred through the centuries by attempting to set such days and hours for the return of Christ, but all have met with disaster. However, their folly should not discourage our faith! ". . . the foundation of God standeth sure. . . . The Lord knoweth them that are his" (2 Timothy 2:19).

With quiet, solemn confidence our Lord declared to His disciples shortly before His crucifixion: "Let not your heart be troubled: ye believe in God, believe also in me. In my Father's house are many mansions: if it *were* not *so,* I would have told you. I go to prepare a place for you. And if I go and prepare a place for you, I will come again, and receive you unto myself; that where I am, there ye may be also" (John 14:1-3).

This promise is described in its glorious fulfillment in so many places in the New Testament that it is hardly necessary to record all of them to establish the fact. We shall, however, mention some of the more prominent ones, so that the great wealth of material on the subject may be both evaluated and appreciated by the reader.

The Apostle Paul, whose inspired pen created a large portion of the literature of the New Testament, consistently reaffirmed the revelation given him by the Savior, which the Apostle termed "the blessed hope, the appearing of the glory of the great God and our Savior, Jesus Christ" (Titus 2:13, literal translation).

In his First Epistle to the Thessalonians, Paul described this moment in the following terms:

> But we do not want to keep you in ignorance, brothers, about those who have fallen asleep, so you may not grieve as others do, who have no hope. For if we believe that Jesus died and arose — well, in similar way God shall bring with Him those who have fallen asleep in Jesus. We tell you this on the Lord's own saying: We, the living who remain at the

coming of the Lord, shall not at all take precedence over those asleep. For with a shout, with the voice of an archangel and the trumpet of God, the Lord shall personally descend from heaven, and those who died in Christ shall rise first. Afterward we, the living who still survive, shall be caught up along with them in the clouds to meet the Lord in the air. And so we shall forever be with the Lord. So then, encourage one another with these words (1 Thessalonians 4:13-18 *Berkeley Version*).

In the foregoing reference it is significant that Paul attaches the return of Jesus Christ to the resurrection of the bodies of all those who have believed in Him throughout all ages. Notice should also be taken of the fact that the spiritual natures (souls or spirits) of those who have died physically while trusting in Christ will be brought back "with Him" (v. 14) to be reunited with their resurrection bodies (see 1 Corinthians 15 for the Apostle Paul's exposition of this fact). So the intermediate state of the redeemed is "with the Lord" (Philippians 1:21-24; 2 Corinthians 5:6-9).

Paul also went to great lengths in his Second Epistle to the Thessalonians to tell them that they should not be "shaken in mind, or be troubled, neither by spirit, nor by word, nor by letter as from us, as that the day of Christ is at hand" (2 Thessalonians 2:2). Instead, he admonishes them not to be deceived "by any means," for the day of the Lord or of Christ will not come upon the Christian church unawares. For, as the apostle put it, ". . . except there come a falling away first, and that man of sin be revealed, the son of perdition; who opposeth and exalteth himself above all that is called God, or that is worshipped; so that he as God sitteth in the temple of God, shewing himself that he is God" (2 Thessalonians 2:3,4).

It should never be forgotten that the day of the Lord and the day of Christ are interchangeable in New Testament Greek, and that deliverance for the church from tribulation is promised at the advent of Jesus Christ, "when the Lord Jesus shall be revealed from heaven with his mighty angels, in flaming fire taking vengeance on them that know not God, and that obey not the gospel of our Lord Jesus Christ: who shall be punished with everlasting destruction from the presence of the Lord, and from the glory of his power; when he shall come to be glorified in his saints, and to be admired in all them that believe (because our testimony among you was believed) in that day" (2 Thessalonians 1:7-10).

A careful study of the twenty-fourth chapter of Matthew's Gospel will reveal that "immediately after the tribulation of those days . . . shall appear the sign of the Son of man in heaven . . . and he shall send his angels with a great sound of a trumpet, and they shall gather together his elect from the four winds from one end of heaven to the other. . . . But as the days of Noe [Noah] *were,* so shall also be the coming of the Son of man. . . . Watch therefore: for ye know not what hour your Lord doth come. . . . Therefore, be ye also ready: for in such an hour as ye think not the Son of Man comes" (Matthew 24:29-31,37, 42,44).

This writer is not particularly interested in discussing the current eschatological mazes which argue about the time of our Lord's return — whether it is *before* the Great Tribulation, in the *middle* of it, or *after* it — or, for that matter, whether the Scripture teaches premillennialism, amillennialism, or postmillennialism. As we noted before, and as the late Dr. Clarence Roddy of Fuller Theological Seminary said: "We have a great enough Lord to take us up or to take us through. It is not so important *when* He is coming as it is *that* He is coming."

THE MULTIPLICATION OF SIGNS

One cannot look upon the restoration and growth of the state of Israel in the twentieth century without being impressed by the fact that the return of the Jews to the land that God gave to Abraham is a unique phenomenon in the history of mankind. The implications of Israel's return cannot escape any careful student of Biblical prophecy, since the destiny of Israel is linked not only with the destiny of the Christian church but, more importantly, with the doctrine of the second advent of Jesus Christ, of whom Pontius Pilate's words now speak with cosmic authority: "This is Jesus of Nazareth, the King of the Jews." Pilate never fully understood what he was somewhat compelled to nail over the Cross of the Nazarene. But it is to his credit that he refused to alter it: "What I have written, I have written," and as it has been written, so shall it come to pass.

It is impossible in the space allotted here to deal fully with those great areas of Biblical prophecy which provide us with signs of the impending arrival of the One into whose hands the Father has committed all judgment, but a brief review will help put the blessed hope of Christians in a clearer perspective for both analysis and understanding.

THE VALLEY OF DEATH AND THE PROMISE OF HOPE
(EZEKIEL 37)

This particular portion of Scripture, written more than 500 years before the birth of Jesus Christ and more than 2,400 years before the rebirth of the state of Israel, is one of the most unique examples of predictive prophecy to be found in the Bible. The prophet is taken out to a valley filled with bones scattered about in disarray, and God asks him the question, "Can these bones live?" (Ezekiel 37:3). The prophet answers that only God can know and then receives a command to "prophesy upon these bones. . . . Ye dry bones, hear the Word of the Lord" (Ezekiel 37:4).

As Ezekiel prophesies, the matching bones come together and are covered with sinews, flesh, and skin, but they have no life in them (v. 8). The prophet is then commanded to prophesy that the Spirit of God may breathe upon the army of the dead lying in the valley of death, "that they may live." We are then told that "breath came into them, and they lived, and stood upon their feet, an exceeding great army" (v. 10).

At this point God interprets the vision which the prophet has seen, and it is a most striking revelation.

Then He said to me: Son of man, these bones are the whole house of
Israel. Yet they continue to say, "Our bones are dried up, our hope is lost,
and we are completely done for!" Therefore prophesy: say to them, Thus
says the Lord God: "Take note! I will open your graves, raise you from
your graves, and bring you into the land of Israel. You shall know that I
am the Lord when I have opened your graves, My people, and brought
you up out of your graves. I will put My Spirit within you, and you shall
live. I will settle you in your own land, and you shall know that I, the
Lord, have said it, and have done it, says the Lord" (Ezekiel 37:11-14
Berkeley Version).

The Lord then continues to show the prophet the restoration
of Israel by causing him to take two sticks, one representing
Joseph and the other Israel. He is commanded to join them
together, and when this is accomplished they miraculously
become one stick in the prophet's hand. The Lord explains to
Ezekiel that when people question what this means, he is to say
to them,

Thus says the Lord God: See, I am about to take the stick of Joseph,
which is in the hand of Ephraim, and the tribes of Israel associated with
him; and I will join with it the stick of Judah, making them a single stick
so that they are united in My hand. Then, holding the sticks, on which
you have written in your hand, before their eyes, say to them, "Thus says
the Lord God: Observe, I am taking the children of Israel from among the
nations where they have gone and will gather them from every quarter
and bring them into their own land; and I will make them one nation in
the land, upon the mountains of Israel. One king shall be king over them
all. They shall no longer be two nations and no longer divided into two
kingdoms. Neither shall they defile themselves any more with their
idols, their foul practices, and all their other transgressions; for I will
save them from all their sinful apostasies and will purify them; so shall
they be My people, and I shall be their God" (Ezekiel 37:19-23 *Berkeley
Version*).

Some critics of the Bible, and of Biblical prophecy in particular, have tried to maintain that this prophecy was written relative
to the return of Israel after the Babylonian captivity. But, as in
the case of most critics, they seldom consider the context very
thoroughly and have omitted serious consideration of verses 24 to
28:

My servant David shall be king over them. They shall all have one shepherd and shall follow My ordinances, obey My statutes, and practice them. They shall dwell in the land which I gave Jacob My servant, the land in which their fathers lived. They shall home in it, they and their children and their children's children forever, and David My servant shall be their prince forever.

I shall make with them a covenant of peace; it shall be for them an everlasting covenant. I will bless them and multiply them, and I will set My sanctuary in the midst of them for all time. My dwelling place shall be with them; I will be their God, and they shall be My people. When my sanctuary remains established among them, then the nations shall know that I, the Lord, sanctify Israel (Ezekiel 37:24-28 *Berkeley Version*).

It is quite obvious to any student of Biblical history that David had been dead for more than 400 years when Ezekiel penned these words from God. So what we are dealing with here is the full restoration of Israel during the millennial kingdom, with a resurrected David reigning under the aegis of His Son, the Messiah, of whom David himself had prophesied (Psalm 110:1).

Israel is indeed returning to her land from among the nations. But they have no "life in them." There is the definite absence of God's Spirit, which can come only when redeemed Israel shall acknowledge the suffering Servant of Isaiah 53, the man from Nazareth.

This part of the prophecy remains unfulfilled, as does the resurrection of David and the establishment of God's sanctuary or temple in Jerusalem (v. 28). But just as the Lord has partially fulfilled this prophecy in our day, the remainder will certainly come to pass, for it is written of Jesus Christ that He is "a light to lighten the Gentiles, and the glory of thy people Israel" (Luke 2:32).

Ezekiel spoke of no temporary restoration of Israel following a period of captivity among other nations. But the supernatural restoration of Israel is mentioned numerous times throughout the Old Testament.

One need only read the following references to recognize that the hope of Israel is indeed the hope of the world. The inauguration of an eternal reign of righteousness is presided over by the Prince of Peace.

THE TESTIMONY OF THE PROPHETS

1. "Behold, I do a new thing; now it is springing forth; do you not recognize it? In the desert I surely will make a way, rivers also in arid wastes" (Isaiah 43:19 *Berkeley Version*).

2. "For I will bring them back to their own land which I gave to their fathers" (Jeremiah 16:14 RSV).

3. "For I will take you from the nations and gather you from all the countries, and bring you into your own land" (Ezekiel 36:24 RSV).

4. " 'I will plant them upon their land, and they shall never again be plucked up out of the land which I have given them,' says the Lord your God" (Amos 9:15 RSV).

5. "For then I will give people a pure language, that all of them may call upon the name of the Lord, to serve Him shoulder to shoulder" (Zephaniah 3:19 *Berkeley Version*).

6. "You, O mountains of Israel, shall shoot forth your branches, and yield your fruit to my people Israel; for they will soon come home" (Ezekiel 36:8 RSV).

7. "And on that day I will seek to destroy all the nations that come against Jerusalem" (Zechariah 12:9 RSV).

8. "And they will say, 'This land that was desolate has become like the garden of Eden' " (Ezekiel 36:35 RSV).

9. "Break forth . . . into singing, you waste places of Jerusalem, for the Lord has comforted His people. He has redeemed Jerusalem" (Isaiah 52:9 RSV).

10. "And the Lord will become king over all the earth; on that day the Lord will be one, and His name one" (Zechariah 14:9 RSV).

11. "In that day Israel will be the third with Egypt and Assyria, a blessing in the midst of the earth" (Isaiah 19:24 RSV).

We can conclude our observations on the blessed hope of the church by pointing out that at our Lord's return in the clouds of heaven (Revelation 1:7) He will appear as lightning (Matthew 24:27), will ransom His church to eternal glory and immortality (1 Thessalonians 4:17), will bring the earth to eternal judgment (2 Peter 3:7-12), will break the power of death over the bodies of Christians (1 Corinthians 15), and will judge the world in righteousness (Acts 17:30,31). That judgment, which after Christ's millennial reign will consummate in eternal justice for Satan and his hosts and the souls of unregenerate men, is a certainty of divine revelation (Revelation 20).

The hope of the ages is more than just the appearance of the son of God, glorious though that will be. The hope of the ages is the restitution of all things — the triumph of sovereign grace over human effort and of good over evil. No longer will sin hold sway over the world of men. No longer will death stalk the sons of Adam. For, as John put it, "It does not yet appear what we shall be, but when He appears we know that we shall be like Him, for we shall see Him as He is" (1 John 3:2 *Berkeley Version*).To be like Jesus Christ is not an empty dream or bravado to be exercised in the presence of death but is instead the glorious outgrowth of the angelic proclamation of that first Easter Day! "He is risen, as He said. Come, see the place where the Lord lay" (Matthew 28:6 *Berkeley Version*).

Let us then watch for His signs, pray for His coming, love His appearing, and hearken to His words, "Behold, I come quickly" and echo, "Even so come, Lord Jesus" (Revelation 22:20). The words of the old hymn ring with ever-increasing intensity, so let us rejoice in them:

> Some golden daybreak Jesus will come,
> Some golden daybreak, battles all won.
> He'll shout the victory — break through the blue —
> Some golden daybreak for me, for you.

10

THE JUDGMENT OF GOD

Of all the doctrines taught in the Bible, none is declared with more consistency and fervor than the doctrine of divine judgment.

Certainly the Scriptures are *filled* with the promises of God's love and mercy and of His apparently inexhaustible patience with the transgression of His creatures. But they *overflow* with His pronouncements of impending judgment upon those who refuse His matchless grace in Jesus Christ.

The certainty of divine judgment takes many forms in the Bible. For instance, Psalm 96:13: ". . . for he cometh, for he cometh to judge the earth: he shall judge the world with righteousness, and the people with his truth." Here the psalmist portrays God intervening in the affairs of the universe and bringing with Him both "righteousness" and "truth," elements totally foreign to man's unregenerate nature. Wise Solomon tells us that God intends to "bring every work into judgment" (Ecclesiastes 12:14), and the prophet Isaiah declares, "The Lord is a God of judgment" (30:18). Indeed, he quotes Jehovah Himself as stating, "I the Lord love judgment, I hate robbery"

(61:8). In such Scriptures God Himself establishes beyond doubt the absolute certainty and inevitability of divine judgment.

Daniel describes the establishment of divine judgment: "The judgment was set, and the books were opened" (7:10). In this awesome picture the Ancient of Days, enthroned among the cherubim and seraphim, pronounces the final decision on a humbled universe — a decision from which there can be no appeal.

Coupled with the Old Testament statements are the clearcut writings of the apostles.

Ending his magnificent discourse on the "unknown god," the Apostle Paul reviews the past patience of God ("The times of this ignorance God overlooked" — Acts 17:30, literal translation) with spiritual power that must have seared to the very depths of his philosophically oriented listeners. Then he declares, "Because he hath appointed a day, in the which he will judge the world in righteousness by *that* man whom he hath ordained; *whereof* he hath given assurance unto all *men*, in that he hath raised him from the dead" (Acts 17:31).

Paul uses such strong words as "assurance," and he re-echoes the promise in Psalm 96 that the world will be judged "in righteousness," a righteousness that will consume the wood, hay, and stubble of a degenerate but religious world.

Paul here links the coming judgment of the world with the Resurrection of Jesus Christ, reinforcing the doctrine taught by our Lord Himself, namely, that "the Father . . . hath committed all judgment unto the Son . . . and hath given him authority to execute judgment also, because he is the Son of man" (John 5:22,27).

The writer of Hebrews emphatically declares, "It is appointed unto men once to die, but after this the judgment" (Hebrews 9:27).

What do all these Scriptures tell us about the judgment? First, God, who cannot lie, has declared that there will be a judgment. Second, this judgment is to encompass all creation. Third, the Judge who will preside is none other than the one like unto the

Son of Man (Daniel 7:13,14; Revelation 1:11-18), who stated in His own words, "As I hear, I judge: and my judgment is just . . . and yet if I judge, my judgment is true. . . . For judgment I am come into this world" (John 5:30; 8:16; 9:39). Of this Judge the angels declared, "Give glory to him; for the hour of his judgment is come" (Revelation 14:7).

No, the matter of judgment cannot be taken lightly, for it introduces the most solemn and foreboding doctrine ever revealed by God.

How many judgments are there? Who will be judged? Here are two more questions that Scripture must answer.

Although some Bible scholars list from three to twelve judgments, many of these judgments are merely phases or parts of judgments. Let us consider some of them.

JUDGMENT AT THE CROSS

At the Cross the Lord Jesus Christ was judged guilty in our stead. God made Him to be sin for us, He who knew no sin, that we might be made as righteous as God by faith in Him (2 Corinthians 5:21). In that sense the sins of the believers were judged in Christ. As a result, the believer is justified fully before God and has passed from death to life. The literal Greek translation of John 5:24 reads, "He that heareth my word, and believeth on him that sent me, hath everlasting life, and shall not come into condemnation; but is passed from death unto life." In Romans 8:1 Paul declares, "There is therefore now no condemnation [judgment unto death] to them which are in Christ Jesus."

We have been freed from the penalty of the law of sin and death and have been acquitted judicially before the throne of God by virtue of the perfect life and vicarious death of Christ.

In *the first judgment*, therefore, the sins of the believer have been fully and finally dealt with at the Cross by Jesus Christ. As the writer of Hebrews tells us, "He had by himself purged our sin" (Hebrews 1:3).

Some groups, such as the Seventh-day Adventists, have not accepted the simplicity of this clear-cut teaching of judgment in the Word of God. Instead, they have introduced what they term "an investigative judgment," a judgment which they teach is now occurring in heaven. Its final outcome, they say, will determine those fit to inherit the kingdom of God. This doctrine is discussed in my book, *The Kingdom of the Cults* (Minneapolis: Bethany Fellowship, 1977). Suffice it to say, however, that John 5:24 disposes of the doctrine of the investigative judgment by declaring that the believer has already passed from death to life by faith in Christ and "shall not come into judgment." This should be clear enough to avoid any misinterpretation.

The second Scriptural judgment is future. It will take place at the return of the Lord Jesus Christ (Matthew 16:27; Luke 14:14; 1 Corinthians 4:4,5; 2 Timothy 4:8; Revelation 22:12), and it will be a judgment of the works of believers. Whatever man has built upon the foundation (Christ), whether it be gold, silver, precious stones, or else wood, hay, and stubble, it must be tried by the fire of divine judgment. But even though a man's works may be consumed, his faith in the imperishable foundation will remain (Matthew 12:36; Romans 14:10; Galatians 6:7; Ephesians 6:8; Colossians 3:24,25; 1 Corinthians 3:11-15).

Paul reminds us that "we must all appear before the judgment seat of Christ" (2 Corinthians 5:10). It should be noted that His counsel is directed to *Christians*, for only the Christian will appear before the judgment *bema* (Greek). This is a judgment for works and has nothing whatever to do with the unsaved. In fact, they are never mentioned in connection with it.

One of the greatest errors ever perpetrated in Christian theology is the erroneous idea that one great judgment will take place at the end of the age, at which all men will be gathered before the Great White Throne. There is absolutely no basis in the Word of God for such an idea.

Although the believer was under judgment by virtue of his Adamic nature (Romans 5:16), in Adam "judgment came upon all men to condemnation," believers have been freed from that condemnation by the sacrifice of Jesus Christ — "by the righteousness of one *the free gift came* upon all men unto justification of life" (Romans 5:18).

GOD JUDGES NATIONS

The third divine judgment taught in the Scripture concerns the righteous judgment of all nations. The Scriptures declare that this judgment will also take place at the return of Jesus Christ (Matthew 25:32). It should be distinguished from the final judgment of the wicked, which takes place at the Great White Throne, since three distinct groups of individuals are represented — "sheep, goats, and brethren." According to verse 31, the setting of this judgment is earth.

Some scholars maintain that the "brethren" are the godly remnant of the Jews who will have been preaching the gospel of Christ throughout the Great Tribulation. Where details are concerned, these things are open to a wide latitude of speculation. But one thing is certain: God intends to judge the nations of the world. Whatever symbolism He may invoke to project this concept, the judgment itself is terrifyingly real.

The fourth judgment in Scripture concerns the nation Israel. Bible scholars may disagree about the nature and extent of this judgment, but they are fairly well agreed that such a judgment must take place. Such passages of Scripture as Ezekiel 20:37,38; Isaiah 1:24-26; Psalm 50:1-7; and Malachi 3:2-5; 4:1,2, definitely teach such a judgment.

Certainly, as Paul puts it, "God hath not cast away his people" (Romans 11:2), but it will be necessary for them to pass through great tribulation so that a godly remnant may be saved out of the wrath which is to come.

The fifth judgment is that of Satan, the beast, the false prophet, and Satan's multitudinous emissaries, the fallen angels. "And the angels which kept not their first estate, but left their own habitation, he hath reserved in everlasting chains under darkness unto the judgment of the great day" (Jude 6). The "great day" is elsewhere called the day of Jehovah, the day of the Lord, or the day of Christ. It signifies that great period of judgment in which God's holiness and righteousness are vindicated and His sentence of eternal wrath is executed.

Jesus once declared, "Now is the judgment of this world: now shall the prince of this world be cast out" (John 12:31). In that statement Satan's doom was sealed. Although sentence was pronounced upon him at the Cross, not until Revelation 20:10 is the sentence executed: "And the devil that deceived them was cast into the lake of fire and brimstone, where the beast and false prophet *are*, and shall be tormented day and night for ever and ever." It is not unreasonable, therefore, to connect the judgment of Satan, the beast, and the false prophet, with the judgment of the fallen angels (2 Peter 2:4; Revelation 20:10). Significantly, according to the Word of God, Christians will be enthroned with Christ, participating in the judgment of angels (1 Corinthians 6:3). We must not forget that Lucifer himself is a fallen angel, one of those whom by God's grace we shall judge. Thus, though we have been tormented by Satan and his emissaries throughout our earthly existence, we shall one day witness the execution of their sentence.

The sixth judgment in the Word of God concerns that of the Great White Throne (Revelation 20:11-15). In this judgment the saints will be seated with Christ, and those "not found in the book of life" will be judged.

The fate of those who endure this judgment is the second death, everlasting separation from the presence of the Lord. These "shall have their part in the lake which burneth with fire and brimstone: which is the second death" (Revelation 21:8).

CHRISTIAN SELF-JUDGMENT

The wonder of the doctrine of divine judgment is the fact that the Christ of Calvary's Cross will be the Judge of the Great White

Throne. What a joy and comfort it is for the believer to realize that he has passed from death to life and will not be judged in the final judgment of the Great White Throne. These facts should cause us as believers to judge ourselves (1 Corinthians 11:31) and admonish ourselves according to Scripture (1 Timothy 1:20; Hebrews 12:7).

The Christian has nothing to fear from these judgments. He need only see that his works be composed of the gold, silver, and precious gems which will endure the fire of God's holiness. Since Peter tells us that "judgment must begin at the house of God" (1 Peter 4:17), we ought to examine ourselves closely, always remembering that "if our heart condemn us, God is greater than our heart, and knoweth all things" (1 John 3:20).

The fruit of divine judgment in the life of the believer is a body dedicated as "a living sacrifice, holy and acceptable to God" (Romans 12:1) and a life filled with the "fruit of the Spirit" dominated in all things by the love which Christ commanded us to have for one another (John 13:35).

On Mars Hill, Paul did not shun from declaring the whole counsel of God to the Athenians. He most certainly assured them of God's love and mercy in Christ, but he also warned them of a divine judgment upon those who would not receive the Lord Jesus Christ, whose Resurrection was the assurance and seal of God's full intention to judge the world in righteousness. This should constantly remind us. This should motivate all of our thoughts as we bear witness for our Lord.

11

THE ERROR OF UNIVERSAL SALVATION

That there are many cults in America today no informed student of contemporary theology can deny. But in addition to the direct problem of non-Christian cults is the disturbing problem of doctrinal deviations within the pale of orthodox Christianity itself. It is with one of these current doctrinal deviations that this chapter is concerned. The deviation is universal reconciliation, or just plain old-fashioned Universalism, which has received a modern rebirth in the theology of Karl Barth. Since the days of Hosea Ballou, the great Universalist preacher of New England, the United States has increasingly become a mecca for the theology of Universalism, or the theory that at the final consummation of the ages God will punish in a *remedial* way the souls of men who have rejected Jesus Christ as Lord and Savior, neither annihilating them nor commiting them to eternal punishment, but rather reconciling them to Himself after a proper period of chastening for their sins. Besides the Unitarian Universalist Church in the United States, which has a waning membership, there are also splinter groups of Universalists, such as the Scripture Studies Concern, located in Corona,

California. Another group of universal reconciliationists is the Concordant Publishing Concern of Los Angeles, formerly headed by A.E. Knoch, a rabid Universalist and also an Arian in the tradition of Jehovah's Witnesses.* These small groups misinterpret a select number of verses found in both the Old and New Testaments. Though almost totally ignorant of the original languages in Scripture, they repeatedly quote for "support" grammatical authorities (mostly out of context) as if their own arguments were based on sound scholarship, which they most decidedly are not. Mr. Knoch, for instance, circulated a "translation" entitled "The Concordant Version," which was the product of his own labors. However, Mr. Knoch admitted that he was neither a Greek nor Hebrew scholar, did not possess degrees in either of the original languages of Scripture, and had his last lessons over fifty years ago! In his translation he attempted to establish Universalism and the Arian doctrine denying the deity of Jesus Christ.

To press on to our real objective in this brief study, we shall now consider some of the basic texts utilized by universal reconciliationists in their attempt to "prove" that the Bible teaches that God intends to save everyone (some have even gone so far as to say that God intends to save the Devil and his angels).

TEXTS MISAPPLIED BY UNIVERSALISTS

Romans 5:18,19. "Therefore as by the offense of one judgment came upon all men to condemnation: even so by the righteousness of one the free gift came upon all men unto justification of life. For as by one man's disobedience many were

---

*Arianism is a form of theology which denies the deity of Jesus Christ and maintains that He was the first and greatest creation of God but not genuine Deity Himself. The Universalist merger (1959) with Unitarianism, a cult which denies the divinity of Christ and the trinity of God, indicates the decline of the theology of the Universalist Church, which was at its inception basically Christian.

made sinners, so by the obedience of one shall many be made righteous."

These first two verses utilized by the universal reconciliationists, when properly understood in their context, in no sense whatsoever teach that salvation is ultimately to be possessed by all men. Quite to the contrary, the Bible clearly teaches that although salvation is offered freely to all men, there are many who just will not accept it! These are the persons of whom Jesus spoke when He said, "Depart from me, ye cursed, into everlasting fire, prepared for the devil and his angels" (Matthew 25:41). Beyond this fact, Paul in the fifth chapter of Romans merely teaches that sin entered the world through one man, Adam. Through this sin the judgment of God came upon all men to eternal death, but God in the fullness of time sent forth His Son, made under the law, to ransom those who had become transgressors through the carnal nature transmitted through Adam. Nowhere does the Scripture say that every man will either now or at some future time (at the prompting of torment) accept this gift; in fact, Christ Himself stated, "O, Jerusalem, Jerusalem, thou that killest the prophets, and stonest them which are sent unto thee, how often would I have gathered thy children together, even as a hen gathereth her chickens under her wings, and ye *would* not!" (Matthew 23:37, emphasis added). It should also be noted that, as the judgment came unto all men to condemnation for sin, the justification of life unto all men was supplied only upon the condition of acceptance of the Lord Jesus Christ as Savior, because justification itself is the result of faith, and faith cometh by hearing, and hearing by the Word of God — conclusive proof indeed that believing the Word of God is the basis for justification before God (Romans 10:17). So we see that the Universalists' argument on the basis of the word "all" melts into nothingness when the context is clearly understood, and when it is realized that the word "all" does not in every instance mean "every"; as a matter of fact, in some instances it is definitely a restrictive term. [For a detailed study of this subject, the reader is referred to A.H. Strong's *Systematic Theology* (Westood, NJ: Revell, 1907), pp. 1047-1056].

Colossians 1:20. "And, having made peace through the blood of his Cross, by him to reconcile all things unto himself; by him, I say, whether they be things in earth or things in heaven."

In this particular text Universalists claim that God will unquestionably reconcile all things to Himself. But the usage of the word "all" is governed by the context, and many times it is definitely not used as a universal, all-inclusive word. While it is definitely true that Christ died to provide a ransom through His blood for all men and that His sacrifice is definitely sufficient for the sins of all men, the Scripture tells us that it is only *efficient* for those who accept it. This is particularly true in the light of John 3:16 and 3:36, where it is stated that God loved the world and commissioned His Son to be its Savior. Therefore, those who accept this sacrifice have everlasting life; those who believe not, the Scripture tells us, "continue to abide under the wrath of God" (John 3:36, literal translation). We are never to forget for a moment that there are two classes of people clearly spoken of in Scripture: the sheep and the goats (Matthew 25:32,33). The sheep are destined for eternal life and the bliss of Christ's eternal presence. The goats, on the other hand, are sentenced to eternal punishment in company with the Devil and his rebellious angels. When Universalists attempt to teach that the reconciliation provided for all men through Calvary will be realized finally by all men, they are, so to speak, whistling in the dark and reading into Scripture what they desperately want the Scripture to teach. No qualified exegetical scholar in the history of the Christian church has ever been able to successfully defend Universalism from the standpoint of the original languages of Scripture. Some men have tried, but they have repeatedly met with failure and theological disaster.

Paul in Colossians never taught that the reconciliation provided by God the Father would eventually be accepted by all men. He only portrayed the grace of God in *providing* redemption, so that *potentially* all men might be saved *if* they repent and accept the gospel. But history tells us that it is not that man *cannot* believe but that he *will not*. "For to be carnally minded is death" (Romans 8:6) — eternal death (or conscious separation from God) — a fact which all Scripture bears out, universal reconciliationists to the contrary notwithstanding.

1 Timothy 4:10. "For therefore we both labour and suffer reproach, because we trust in the living God, who is the Saviour of all men, specially of those that believe."

To argue that this text irrevocably teaches that God intends to save all men is exegetical folly. The text itself states nothing of the sort. It is very true that God's *desire* is that all men should be saved. He could not be a loving God unless His desire was that His creations be delivered from the fruit of their own wickedness, but the text does not say that all men *will* be saved; rather, it teaches that God in the measureless depths of His eternal love has made *provision* for their salvation, a provision which some of them will *never* accept. First Timothy 2:4 is used in connection with this text, incidentally, although it also gives no sound exegetical ground for supposing that God has decreed immutably that all mankind shall be saved. This assertion simply is not true! If our universal-salvation friends would study the second half of 1 Timothy 4:10, they would find that Paul qualifies his use of the term "all" by stating "specially of those that believe," so we see that while God is the Savior of all men in the *potential* sense of the term, He is *actually* the Savior only of those who believe and accept Jesus Christ as Lord and Savior. The emphatic statement of Christ to Nicodemus in John 3:3 is as true today as when he uttered it almost 2,000 years ago: "Except a man be born again, he cannot see the kingdom of God." All the Universalist argument in the world cannot change the fact that if a man rejects the sacrificial blood of Jesus Christ, apart from which there is no remission for sin (Hebrews 9:22), then he most certainly cannot be cleansed by fire. This method of cleansing is espoused by some Universalists, who affirm that God will punish for many "eons" of time the unrepentant souls of men until they will see the evil of their rejection of Christ and accept Him finally as Lord and Savior, thus meriting salvation. Such a view as this predicates in effect "salvation by suffering," and the Bible clearly teaches that it is only the blood of Jesus Christ God's Son that cleanses us from all sin (1 John 1:7) — not the suffering of the soul, regardless of its intensity or duration.

A fourth and final text seized upon by Universalists to buttress their claims for universal reconciliation is *1 Corinthians 15:28* — "And when all things shall be subdued unto him, then shall the Son also himself be subject unto him that put all things under him, that God may be all in all."

From this passage of Scripture the Universalists assume that because God will eventually become all in all, the "all" must refer to everything in creation which possesses a spiritual nature — men, angels, etc. However, they neglect to read the context in which Paul is speaking, for in this chapter the Apostle states clearly that only the *redeemed* are to be transformed into the likeness of Christ after their resurrection to immortality, and nowhere in the chapter is there the vaguest suggestion that the "all" spoken of refers to anyone but those raised in the image of Christ, i.e., the regenerated and redeemed souls of believers. Reconciliationists also couple this text with verse 22 of the same chapter, "For as in Adam all die, even so in Christ shall all be made alive," in a vain attempt to establish the impossible tenet that as spiritual death came to Adam through sin and so passed upon all men, so God in Christ intends to make all men spiritually alive. That this position is Biblically untenable can easily be seen by a study of this context in the original Greek. The context clearly indicates that it is one of resurrection — a direct reference to resurrection and resurrection only, and to capture the sense of the Greek properly it should be rendered, "As in Adam all die, so in Christ shall all be raised to life" (or "resurrected"). This we know to be true because there will be a resurrection of the just and of the unjust (Acts 24:15). Therefore, since this is the case, the ground which Universalists stand upon is the weakest possible type, for when all the tools of proper Biblical study are employed in the evaluation of their textual arguments, not *one* of their positions can successfully stand the test.

It is not possible to list all the verses utilized by universal reconciliationists to establish their unbiblical premises, but the above cross section should serve to demonstrate the danger of building doctrines upon isolated words with little or no consideration of context or the related background of the language both grammatically and exegetically.

SCRIPTURE STUDIES CONCERN

We might mention at this time a certain sect of zealous Bible students who group themselves under the title listed above. This small organization publishes a series of pamphlets, many of which are written or edited by zealous universal reconciliationists. To all appearances this group is sound on the basic issues of the gospel but finds itself unable to accept the doctrine of eternal retribution for sin. As a result of this, it has circulated many pamphlets attempting to prove that everlasting punishment is *not* Biblical and that the Bible *teaches* universal reconciliation. One of its pamphlets, entitled *The Bible and the Cross*, is a cleverly edited compilation from the writings of Rev. G. Campbell Morgan and Rev. W. H. Griffith Thomas, copied from the *Presbyterian* of June 1932. Unfortunately, the Scripture Studies Concern, in its zeal to establish universal reconciliation, has employed some highly questionable methods and ethics, for the editors have deliberately deleted sentences and skipped paragraphs in an attempt to make it appear that Drs. Morgan and Thomas endorsed their position! However, anyone familiar with the writings of these men realizes almost at once that they never held such a position at all.

In line with many deviant groups, the Scripture Studies Concern has seized upon out-of-context quotations from recognized expositors of a conservative position to add prestige to their highly questionable interpretations of Scripture. They have not told the whole truth, and their publications should be viewed with great suspicion by watchful Christians.

This small sect also utilizes another trait found in many cults. In a supposed emphasis upon exegesis from the original languages of Scripture, individuals who are hardly qualified to read technical exegetical books continually pose as scholars of the original languages! On pages 13 and 14 of the pamphlet *The Bible and the Cross*, published by this group, the author goes into great detail on the meaning of the Greek noun *aion* (eon), which she states confidently cannot possibly mean "without end." This argument stems from the old chestnut perpetually turned over in the fires of theological debate, which all qualified Greek scholars recognize as merely a "dodge" to escape the paralyzing reality that the Greek language teaches in no uncertain terms *eternal punishment* for sin. (If the statement is true, incidentally, then Romans 16:26 teaches beyond a question of a doubt that Almighty God Himself has an end in time — at the end of an *aion* or eons, periods of time during which specific things are carried out according to the will of God!) The comparison of the usage of the word *aionion* as it is used in the Greek New Testament would show the interested reader immediately that in numerous contexts the word means "everlasting" or "forever."

To quote Dr. William Pettingill: "When the Scriptures speak of everlasting hills or everlasting earthly arrangements or processes, of everlasting doors and chairs, of burning or fire or of punishment by destruction, or of any transient thing, the word is limited by the nature of the thing spoken of and by the common sense of those to whom they speak. There is no need of misunderstanding their meaning." With this statement we agree, but as Dr. Strong has so clearly pointed out in a devastating chapter on everlasting punishment (see Strong's *Systematic Theology*, pp. 1047 ff.), the term *aionion* or *aionas* appears in the same context in Matthew's Gospel referring to the condition of the saved as does Christ's reference to the damned: "And these shall go away into everlasting punishment: but the righteous into life eternal" (Matthew 25:46). Therefore, if we would limit the duration of the punishment of the damned, then by all the laws of sound exegesis we must limit the eternal habitation of the saved! This far even no universal reconciliationist is willing to go!

There are, of course, contexts in the New Testament where the words *aionion* or *aionas* are found where they could not possibly refer to eternal things. However, the context clearly determines their meanings, and for universal reconciliationists to claim on the basis of a Greek noun or adjectival form that the Bible does not teach everlasting retribution when the overwhelming majority of Greek scholars — classical and koine — have taught historically the direct opposite is just one more evidence of their lack of scholastic resources.

The danger of Universalism or universal reconciliation is that one may be led to believe that if God intends to save everyone, then we can afford to be lax both in our Chrisitian lives and in our zeal to proclaim the riches of the gospel. The real key as to why universal reconciliationists cannot accept eternal punishment is that they are pure rationalists. To this fact the aforementioned pamphlet bears irrefutable evidence, for, as the author says: "We cannot conceive of a Creator who knows the end from the beginning, one who is love, who has infinite wisdom and infinite power, giving to any being life, life which is never to end, but continue in suffering to all eternity. The Bible does not teach it anywhere in the original language. God's punishments are remedial and take place within the span of the ages during which He is accomplishing the making of man in His image and likeness. Punishment will last no longer than is necessary to bring man to hate his sin and be reconciled to his Savior" (*The Bible and the Cross*, p. 14).

We see, therefore, that merely because universal reconciliationists cannot conceive of God punishing eternally the infinite sin of rejecting His Son, they have sought to draw from Scripture what neither scholarship nor common sense can possibly allow. Since they cannot conceive of God so punishing the unregenerate soul, they have set up their own standard of how God *must* act based upon what *they* believe is justice. The juggling of the Greek terms for "everlasting" and "eternal" by persons who are not recognized scholastic authorities is one more evidence of the paucity of their resources. Even F. W. Farrar, the great and noble historian and minister of the gospel who was himself a brilliant Greek scholar and a friend of Universalism, could not bring himself to pervert the grammar of the New Testament. He believed that everlasting meant everlasting, especially in the contexts relative to the redeemed and the lost.

In concluding this chapter we ought always to fix in our minds these three facts: (1) the grammar of the New Testament teaches that there will be everlasting bliss for those who accept Jesus Christ as Lord and Savior (John 5:24, 6:47, etc.); (2) this same grammar teaches, with the same words, in the same syntactical form, and many times in the same context, that there will be everlasting punishment for those who willfully reject Jesus Christ as Lord and Savior (John 3:36; Matthew 25:32,33; Revelation 20:10; etc.); and (3) salvation from sin has been provided for all men through the blood of the Cross (1 John 2:2), and whosoever will may come, according to the will of God, who orders all things after the counsel of His own will. But that God knows and has declared in His Word that many will not accept His provision of redemption and will in fact trample under foot the blood of Jesus, no qualified scholar denies. These are the persons clearly described in Scripture, those "whose end is destruction, whose God is their belly" (Philippians 3:19), "raging waves of the sea, foaming out their own shame; wandering stars, to whom is reserved the blackness of darkness forever" (Jude 13).

If we keep these three cardinal points before us, recognizing that the Scriptures as a unit teach these truths whether or not we can accept them on a rationalistic basis or whether or not we can understand the character of God this side of eternity, we shall protect ourselves from the error of universal reconciliation and of Universalism itself. This is the error which has plagued the Christian church since the days of Origen, and which has laid the groundwork for many more heresies, since this form of theology has the tendency to lead the unwary further into fields of doctrinal deviation.

Let us, then, heed the Apostle Paul, and faithfully "put on the whole armour of God, that ye may be able to stand against the wiles of the devil" (Ephesians 6:11).

12

THE UNANSWERABLE ARGUMENT

Theologians through the centuries have devised various arguments to prove the existence of God, the validity of Christianity, and the certainty of divine judgment. Added to these are arguments designed to show the uniqueness of Jesus Christ, His perfect life, and His miraculous powers. Prophetic evidence concerning Christ from the Old Testament and its fulfillment in the New Testament is also introduced as a powerful argument for the acceptance of the Christian message.

Our preceding survey of key Biblical doctrines has presented and underscored the importance of a solid foundation for faith. But, as we previously pointed out, the affirmation of doctrine *alone* is insufficient. While revelation is primary, it receives far greater support and validation in the eyes of men when it is confirmed in personal experience than when it is merely postulated, affirmed, or accepted by faith. It is with this aspect, the experiential confirmation of Christianity, that we are concerned in this closing chapter.

We would certainly not minimize the importance of doctrinal truth or of theological arguments for the validity of the Christian religion, but, taking all these things into account and granting that they have their place, we must still admit that they are not unanswerable. One has only to remember the deluge of material from the pens of unbelieving philosophers, scientists, and liberal theologians who reject many, if not all, of the postulates of historic Christianity.

Alternate explanations for the existence of the universe are abundant in scientific circles today, and we are being told that belief in God and the supreme moral laws ordained by Him are not necessary for an ethical, moral, and generally wholesome existence.

Frequently, when a Christian attempts to bear witness for his Lord, he meets a host of objections based supposedly on science and logic. In the end he must rely primarily upon the Scriptures. If they are denied as an authoritative revelation, he finds himself driven to the last citadel — personal experience. However, when he gives testimony to his relationship with Christ, he is told that this is subjectivism and that others have had similar experiences in other religions. Why must he consider his the only authoritative experience?

This line of reasoning frustrates many Christians who do not realize that there is an unanswerable argument. Strangely enough, this argument is fashioned from the same material that the unbeliever has apparently used to challenge effectively the Christian message. Let me illustrate what I mean with a Biblical example.

In the ninth chapter of the Gospel of John, our Lord healed a man born blind, whose afflictions were the direct result of God's will, that through the healing God might be glorified and Christ's Messianic office established. Almost immediately after this miraculous healing the enemies of Jesus attempted to intimidate the man and his parents. First, they questioned whether or not it was the same man. Then, upon learning that the healing was genuine, they set about slandering Christ, urging the man to "give God the praise: we know that this man is a sinner" (v. 24).

The answer of the blind man is classic: "Whether he be a sinner or no, I know not: *one thing I know, that, whereas I was blind, now I see.* . . . Why herein is a marvellous thing, that ye know not from whence he is, and yet he hath opened mine eyes. Now we know that God heareth not sinners: but if any man be a worshipper of God, and doeth his will, him he heareth. Since the world began was it not heard that any man opened the eyes of one that was born blind. If this man were not of God, he could do nothing" (vv. 25, 30-33, emphasis added).

The blind man was certain of a very real experience, an existential fact, to use the language of modern philosophy. He had been blind, and now he could see. Jesus Christ had made the difference, and no amount of argument on the part of the Pharisees or scribes could shake him.

The pages of history are filled with cases like that of the blind man. Here is evidence validated by time and close scrutiny by hostile eyes. Despite all of the persecutions, mockery, and rejection which have been heaped upon the followers of Christ, the unbeliever is awed by the majesty of a faith that will not die because it does what no other faith has ever done: it transforms men into the image of God.

Here is no merely subjective argument but demonstrable fact. The good news of God's love in Christ is credited by all transformed persons with being the origin and sustaining force of that transforming experience. This alone explains why they have such love for Him and why they are willing both to live and die in His service.

The Apostle Paul put it another way: "I am crucified with Christ: nevertheless I live; yet not I, but Christ liveth in me: and the life which I now live in the flesh I live by the faith of the Son of God, who loved me, and gave himself for me" (Galatians 2:20).

The secular and scientific age in which we live demands that things be tested and re-tested. They require evidence upon evidence, fact upon fact. Yet here in the truest sense is a controlled experiment. Christianity has been observed for almost two thousand years. Wherever it is faithfully proclaimed, accepted, and acted upon, it transforms men, cultures, and societies; and it can do this only because it is energized by a living Savior.

The Son of God is unique not only by virtue of fact that He is the incarnate Word of God and the risen Redeemer, but also because He is the Regenerator of twisted and tormented souls. The alcoholic, the drug addict, the prostitute, the confused, the frustrated, and the despairing respond alike to the voice of the Savior. Whereas once they were blind, now they see. This miraculous force that is imparted to those who have been found by Christ transforms the alcoholic into a model of sobriety, the prostitute into a faithful housewife and mother, the drug addict into a useful member of the community, and men and women in every degree of spiritual and moral disintegration into new creations.

Inscribed upon the tomb of the great architect Christopher Wren is this statement, "If you would see the man's monument, look around." Well might we say this is an infinitely greater sense of Jesus Christ, for through the centuries He has established living monuments to His power to save, miraculously transforming the lives of those who would dare to believe the incredible.

Men may devise every form of argument to establish the certainty of God and the claims of Christianity, but the unanswerable argument in all its simple splendor remains ever before us if we will but grasp its significance. The world can offer no alternative explanation to the divine memorial of a transformed life.

The blind man of John's Gospel had grasped this great truth. The answer of the unbelievers was, then as now, blind reprisal and denunciation followed by significant silence in the face of the incontrovertible fact of experience.

Let us understand clearly at this juncture that a person may "change" in his attitudes and way of life apart from Christian redemption (witness the atheistic or non-Christian alcoholic who "reforms" or the person converted to non-Christian religions or cults who reverses his or her course of action totally apart from the Christian imperative).

Does this mean that his experience is a genuine regeneration of the soul and a reconciliation to God because he has had an "experience" which affected his life for the better? The answer to this is that we must understand the motivation for his "reformation" before we can evaluate its content and value.

Since all religions except Christianity emphasize man's capacity to save himself by either atoning for his sins or reforming his life to "balance the books" of divine justice, the solution to non-Christian conversion experiences is readily discernible. In the case of an atheist he may change because of the pressures of society or the obligations of family or job, or out of a desire to better his condition. In the case of converts to a non-Christian religion or cult, experience has shown that they previously possessed little spiritual depth and never held strong allegiance to their previous faith. Hence there was very little religious persuasion from which they needed to be converted. In a great percentage of cases they existed in a spiritual vacuum, having rejected the historic gospel of Jesus Christ and having settled instead for an inferior substitute in an attempt to fill the vacuum. Of course, there are exceptions which would need to be explained in greater depth in light of the circumstances surrounding the individual case, but by and large such "converts" have no real consciousness of sin or of alienation from the life of God or of their need for reconciliation and subjection to the Father of spirits (Hebrews 12:9). Neither class of people changes *because* they have become aware of their lost condition before a holy God and have come to realize their desperate need of spiritual cleansing from the results and penalty of sin. Such persons never confess their total inability to save themselves. Rather, their so-called conversion experience and the change in their lives that follows it is for them the direct *means of* their self-redemption spiritually, physically, socially, or economically.

The motivation for such non-Christian, counterfeit experiences is self-salvation, or the attempt to extricate oneself from the mire of sin by tugging vigorously at the bootstraps of self-reformation and good works. On the other hand, a Christian conversion is quite the opposite; the motivation is totally different. A person who accepts Jesus Christ accepts Him as his only hope of deliverance from the shackles of sin, pride, and self-justification. True conversion is based upon the realization that one is bereft of any spiritual content sufficient to justify the soul before the laws of a holy Deity. And the transforming change that takes place is the result of a God-given desire to show one's love and gratitude for a free gift (forgiveness and redemption) beyond the reach of any human effort apart from saving grace (Ephesians 2:8-10).

The motivation for the "new life" that is lived is love for God in Christ and a desire to please Him and share His salvation and its attendant attitudes, blessings, and fruits with others.

The counterfeit can be detected only when it is properly contrasted with the original. The key to its correct identification is motivation, a good subject to explore when faced with "conversions" and "reformed lives" that reject the Word of God and Jesus Christ — God's *only* method for making men holy (John 14:6).

Let us not be deceived by other religions which claim the power to redemptively alter lives. Above all, let us not fear honest investigation of either our doctrines or our Christian experience by other religions, modern science, or higher education.

We have nothing to fear from higher education, and every step that science takes vindicates the record of Scripture. Archeology has established the accuracy of the Word of God. Psychology has validated the structure of man's immaterial nature. Physics confirms the laws governing the universe. Astronomy testifies to the enormity of God's power. In every branch of science men are beginning to see the emerging outline of a Mind and purpose so gigantic and complex that it staggers the imagination. In the light of all this, let us not surrender; let us gird ourselves for that which lies ahead. Let us look with confidence toward that day when "at the name of Jesus every knee shall bend and every tongue shall confess that He is Lord to the glory of God the Father" and "the kingdoms of this world" will indeed become "the kingdoms of our Lord, and of his Christ" (Revelation 11:15).

Until that promised and certain consummation, the Mary Magdalenes, the blind men, the Sauls, the Augustines, and the countless millions of spiritual lepers transformed by the power of the Son of God remain a spiritual challenge and question mark that the world, for all its wisdom, can neither refute nor adequately explain. The Scripture speaks truth indeed when it says: "Therefore if any man be in Christ, he is a new creature: old things are passed away; behold, all things are become new" (2 Corinthians 5:17.)

To the skeptic and the unbeliever who, like Nathaniel of old, doubt that "we have found him, of whom Moses in the law, and the prophets, did write" (John 1:45), we echo the invitation of Philip, "Come and see" (John 1:46).

There can be no doubt that if men will "reason together" (Isaiah 1:18) with the Lord and "call ye upon him while he is near" (Isaiah 55:6), they will find Him if they seek Him with all their hearts.

He who knows the plight of the sparrow (Matthew 10:29) and the need of the young ravens (Luke 12:24) and who numbers the hairs of the head (Matthew 10:30) surely knows the longing of our souls, for He is "not far from every one of us. For in him we live, and move, and have our being" (Acts 17:27,28).

To those who come to Him, Jesus Christ becomes the solution to all the problems of soul and body. The results of their experience with Him become the truly unanswerable argument of essential Christianity.